Timeless Quotations on

LIVING ONE
DAY AT A TIME

Love from

Celeste

POCKET POSITIVES™

Timeless Quotations on

LIVING
ONE DAY
AT A TIME

Compiled by John Cook

Fairview Press
Minneapolis

Published by Fairview Press, 2450 Riverside Avenue South, Minneapolis, MN 55454.

Library of Congress Cataloging-in-Publication Data
Timeless quotations on living one day at a time /
    compiled by John Cook.
        p.   cm. -- (Pocket positives)
    ISBN 1-57749-058-4 (pbk.: alk. paper)
    1. Conduct of life--Quotations, maxims, etc.
    2. Life--Quotations, maxims, etc. 3. Affirmations.
    I. Cook, John, 1939–   . II. Series.
    BJ1581.2.T54   1997
    158.1--dc21   97-31317'
First Printing: November 1997   CIP
Printed in the United States of America
01 00 99 98 97   7 6 5 4 3 2 1

Cover design: Laurie Duren

Publisher's Note: The publications of Fairview Press, including the Pocket Positives™ series, do not necessarily reflect the philosophy of Fairview Health System or its treatment programs.

For a free catalogue, call toll-free 1–800–544–8207 or visit our web site at www.press.fairview.org.

for Freddi, Blake, Brian, and Timmy

CONTENTS

Introduction, ix

Part One: *One Day,* 1

Part Two: *Yesterday: The Past,* 69

Part Three: *Today: The Present,* 97

Part Four: *This Moment,* 133

Part Five: *Mornings,* 143

Part Six: *Evenings,* 165

Part Seven: *Tomorrow: The Future,* 175

Part Eight; *Average Days,* 191

Part Nine: *Difficult Days,* 205

Part Ten: *One Step at a Time,* 225

INTRODUCTION

THE BOOKS IN THE POCKET POSITIVES™ SERIES originated as a selection of life-affirming quotations I compiled for my nephews and niece for Christmas 1989.

Because I was concerned that one of them was too young for it, I wrote in a letter that accompanied the collection, "just put it away in a safe place until you're ready for it." To address the question of how someone would know they were "ready," I wrote:

"You'll be ready the first time things don't go the way you want them to, the first time you doubt your ability to do something, the first time you're tempted to quit or give up, the first time you actually fail at something.

"You'll be ready the first time you doubt a friend, or think you can't trust anyone.

"You'll be ready the first time you have to make an important decision, or choice.

"You'll be ready the first time you're afraid of something, or worried.

"You'll know when you're ready. When you are, these thoughts should give you the courage and confidence and spirit you need ... and they'll remind you of the wonder and the joy of life, regardless of how dark things seem at the moment.

"I know they will.... They always have for me."

So, in addition to being a resource for researchers, writers, students, and professionals, I hope this book—and all the books in the Pocket Positives™ series—will provide comfort and inspiration for the casual browser or reader.

• • •

Numerous questions and concerns about accuracy confront anyone who compiles quotations. Take, for example, differences in the spelling of sources' names. The same famous Russian novelist has had his name spelled "Dostoevski," "Dostoievski," and "Dostoyevsky."

The formality required to identify sources is another issue. The Spanish Jesuit writer Baltasar Gracian Y Morales, for example, is more commonly referred to as "Baltasar Gracian," or simply "Gracian." And some sources are almost universally referred to by only one name, usually in the interest of brevity, and because it would be difficult to confuse them with anyone else. "Crebillion," for example, is used for Prosper Jolyot de Crebillion, the French dramatic poet.

And, of course, through the years many exact quotations—and even more that are very similar—have been attributed to more than one source.

I have made every effort to present each quotation as accurately as possible, and to recognize and honor the appropriate source. In particularly demanding situations, the language and sources cited are those most often used by other compilers and editors. Where it was impossible to verify the accuracy or source of a quotation, I have included it anyway if I believed that the usefulness of the quotation outweighed the demands of scholarly rigor.

PART ONE

ONE DAY

It's Impossible to Overstate the Value of One Day

No one can confidently say that he will still be living tomorrow.

—Euripides

Nothing is worth more than this day.

—Johann von Goethe

What a folly to dread the thought of throwing away life at once, and yet have no regard to throwing it away by parcels and piecemeal.

—John Howe

Not a day passes over this earth but men and women of note do great deeds, speak great words and suffer noble sorrows.

—Charles Reed

We create our fate every day we live.

—Henry Miller

Who loses a day loses life.
　　　　　　　—Ralph Waldo Emerson

May you live all the days of your life.
　　　　　　　—Jonathan Swift

If we only knew the real value of a day.
　　　　　　　—Joseph Farrell

We are involved in a life that passes
understanding: our highest business is
our daily life.
　　　　　　　—John Cage

We die daily. Happy those who daily
come to life as well.
　　　　　　　—George MacDonald

He who has lived a day has lived an age.
　　　　　　　—Jean de La Bruyere

Life, we learn too late, is in the living, in
the tissue of every day and hour.
　　　　　　　—Stephen Leacock

To sensible men, every day is a day of reckoning.

—John W. Gardner

A day's impact is better than a month of dead pull.

—Oliver Wendell Holmes

The proper function of man is to live, not to exist. I shall not waste my days in trying to prolong them.

—Jack London

A day, an hour, of virtuous liberty is worth a whole eternity in bondage.

—Joseph Addison

While we live, let us live.

—D.H. Lawrence

Gladly accept the gifts of the present hour.

—Horace

There is but a step between me and death.

—1 Sm. 20:3

They deem me mad because I will not sell my days for gold; and I deem them mad because they think my days have a price.

—Kahlil Gibran

Live mindful of how brief your life is.

—Horace

Everyone once, once only. Just once and no more. And we also once. Never again.

—Rainer Maria Rilke

Most of us spend our lives as if we had another one in the bank.

—Ben Irwin

It's better to be a lion for a day than a sheep all your life.

—Sister Elizabeth Kenny

No objects of value ... are worth risking
the priceless experience of waking up one
more day.

—Jack Smith

Every possession and every happiness is
but lent by chance for an uncertain time,
and may therefore be demanded back the
next hour.

—Arthur Schopenhauer

Some days you tame the tiger. And some
days the tiger has you for lunch.

—Tug McGraw

So teach us to number our days, that we
may apply our hearts unto wisdom.

—Ps. 90:12

You have got to own your days and live
them, each one of them, every one of
them, or else the years go right by and
none of them belong to you.

—Herb Gardner

The ideal never comes. Today is ideal for him who makes it so.

—Horatio W. Dresser

True wisdom lies in gathering the precious things out of each day as it goes by.

—E.S. Bouton

The most important thing in our lives is what we are doing now.

—Anon.

Write it on your heart that every day is the best day in the year.

—Ralph Waldo Emerson

He possesses dominion over himself, and is happy, who can every day say, "I have lived." Tomorrow the heavenly Father may either involve the world in dark clouds, or cheer it with clear sunshine; he will not, however, render ineffectual the things which have already taken place.

—Horace

The days come and go like muffled and veiled figures sent from a distant friendly party, but they say nothing, and if we do not use the gifts they bring, they carry them as silently away.

—Ralph Waldo Emerson

Your daily life is your temple and your religion.

—Kahlil Gibran

He is only rich who owns the day. There is no king, rich man, fairy, or demon who possesses such power as that.

—Ralph Waldo Emerson

Life is now ... this day, this hour ... and is probably the only experience of the kind one is to have.

—Charles Macomb Flandrau

Each day, each hour, an entire life.

—Juan Ramon Jimenel

The Value of Time

Nothing is ours except time.
>—Marcus Annaeus Seneca

Nothing in business is so valuable as time.
>—John H. Patterson

Possessions dwindle: I mourn their loss. But I mourn the loss of time much more, for anyone can save his purse, but none can win back lost time.
>—Latin proverb

Riches are chiefly good because they give us time.
>—Charles Lamb

One realizes the full importance of time only when there is little of it left. Every man's greatest capital asset is his unexpired years of productive life.
>—Paul W. Litchfield

Our costliest expenditure is time.
—Theophrastus

Know the true value of time; snatch,
seize, and enjoy every moment of it. No
idleness, no laziness, no procrastination:
never put off till tomorrow what you can
do today.
—Lord Chesterfield

Gather ye rose-buds while ye may,
Old time is still a-flying.
And this same flower that smiles today,
Tomorrow will be dying.
—Henry David Thoreau

Many people take no care of their money
till they come nearly to the end of it, and
others do just the same with their time.
—Johann von Goethe

All my possessions for a moment of time.
—Queen Elizabeth I

Let me tell thee, time is a very precious gift of God; so precious that it's only given to us moment by moment.
—Amelia Barr

A sense of the value of time ... is an essential preliminary to efficient work; it is the only method of avoiding hurry.
—Arnold Bennett

Pick my left pocket of its silver dime, but spare the right—it holds my golden time!
—Oliver Wendell Holmes

Lost time is never found again.
—Benjamin Franklin

We work not only to produce, but to give value to time.
—Eugene Delacroix

As every thread of gold is valuable, so is every moment of time.
—John Mason

Minutes are worth more than money.
Spend them wisely.

>—Thomas P. Murphy

Time is the coin of your life. It is the only
coin you have, and only you can determine how it will be spent. Be careful lest
you let other people spend it for you.

>—Carl Sandburg

Dollars cannot buy yesterday.

>—Admiral Harold R. Stark

If a person gives you his time, he can
give you no more precious gift.

>—Frank Tyger

You may ask me for anything you like
except time.

>—Napoleon Bonaparte

Time is the most valuable thing a man
can spend.

>—Laertius Diogenes

The laboring man and the artificer
knows what every hour of his time is
worth, and parts not with it but for the
full value.

—Lord Clarendon

Time isn't a commodity, something you
pass around like cake. Time is the substance of life. When anyone asks you to
give your time, they're really asking for a
chunk of your life.

—Antoinette Bosco

Don't be fooled by the calendar. There
are only as many days in the year as you
make use of. One man gets only a week's
value out of a year while another man
gets a full year's value out of a week.

—Charles Richards

Every minute of life carries with it its
miraculous value, and its face of eternal
youth.

—Albert Camus

Love and time—those are the only two things in all the world and all of life that cannot be bought, but only spent.

—Gary Jennings

There is nothing good in this world which time does not improve.

—Alexander Smith

The great rule of moral conduct is, next to God, to respect Time.

—Johann Kaspar Lavater

It is the time you have wasted for your rose that makes your rose so important.

—Antoine de Saint-Exupery

One hour of life, crowded to the full with glorious action and filled with noble risks, is worth whole years of those mean observances of paltry decorum.

—Sir Walter Scott

THE IMPORTANCE OF
USING TIME WELL

Seize the hour.

—Sophocles

During a very busy life I have often been
asked, "How did you manage to it all?"
The answer is very simple: it is because I
did everything promptly.

—Sir Richard Tangye

I must govern the clock, not be governed
by it.

—Golda Meir

The organized person ... makes the most
of his time and goes to his bed for the
night perfectly relaxed for rest and
renewal.

—George Matthew Adams

Seize time by the forelock.

—Pittacus of Mitylene

Time cannot be expanded, accumulated, mortgaged, hastened, or retarded.

—Anon.

Time is a tyranny to be abolished.

—Eugene Jolus

We must use time as a tool, not as a crutch.

—John F. Kennedy

He who every morning plans the transactions of the day and follows out that plan carries a thread that will guide him through the labyrinth of the most busy life.... If the disposal of time is surrendered merely to the chance of incident, chaos will soon reign.

—Victor Hugo

The time which we have at our disposal every day is elastic; the passions that we feel expand it, those that we inspire contract it; and habit fills up the rest.

—Marcel Proust

The ability to concentrate and to use
time well is everything.

—Lee Iacocca

Have a time and place for everything,
and do everything in its time and place,
and you will not only accomplish more,
but have far more leisure than those who
are always hurrying.

—Tyron Edwards

Time is an equal opportunity employer.
Each human being has exactly the same
number of hours and minutes every day.
Rich people can't buy more hours.
Scientists can't invent new minutes. And
you can't save time to spend it on another day. Even so, time is amazingly fair
and forgiving. No matter how much
time you've wasted in the past, you still
have an entire tomorrow. Success
depends upon using it wisely—by planning and setting priorities.

—Denis Waitely

An Italian philosopher said that "time was his estate"; an estate indeed which will produce nothing without cultivation, but will always abundantly repay the labors of industry, and generally satisfy the most extensive desires, if no part of it be suffered to lie in waste by negligence, to be overrun with noxious plants, or laid out for show rather than for use.

—Samuel Johnson

Timely service, like timely gifts, is doubled in value.

—George MacDonald

Time is the one thing that can never be retrieved.

—C.R. Lawton

Make use of time, let not advantage slip.

—William Shakespeare

O, for an engine to keep back all clocks!

—Ben Johnson

WASTING TIME

I wish I could stand on a busy corner,
hat in hand, and beg people to throw me
all their wasted hours.

—Bernard Berenson

Wasted time means wasted lives.

—R. Shannon

Regret for time wasted can become a
power for good in the time that remains,
if we will only stop the waste and the
idle, useless regretting.

—Arthur Brisbane

I wasted time, and now doth time waste
me.

—William Shakespeare

All that time is lost which might be better employed.

—Jean-Jacques Rousseau

Lost, yesterday, somewhere between sunrise and sunset, two golden hours, each set with sixty diamond minutes. No reward is offered, for they are gone forever.

—Horace Mann

Thrift of time will repay you in afterlife, with a usury of profit beyond your most sanguine dreams; waste of it will make you dwindle, alike in intellectual and moral stature, beyond your darkest reckoning.

—William Gladstone

The clock upbraids me with the waste of time.

—William Shakespeare

Time is lost when we have not lived a full human life, time unenriched by experience, creative endeavor, enjoyment, and suffering.

—Dietrich Bonhoeffer

Does't thou love life? Then do not squander time, for that is the stuff life is made of.

—Benjamin Franklin

Time wasted is a theft from God.

—Henri Frederic Amiel

Lost time is like a run in a stocking. It always gets worse.

—Ann Morrow Lindbergh

As if you could kill time without injuring eternity.

—Henry David Thoreau

Killing time is the chief end of our society.

—Ugo Betti

No person will have occasion to complain of the want of time who never loses any.

—Thomas Jefferson

Time is that which man is always trying
to kill, but which ends in killing him.
—Herbert Spencer

Men talk of killing time, while time quietly kills them.
—Dion Boucicault

Modern man thinks he loses something—time—when he does not do
things quickly. Yet he does not know
what to do with the time he gains—
except kill it.
—Erich Fromm

A man who dares to waste one hour of
life has not discovered the value of life.
—Charles Darwin

If time be of all things most precious,
wasting time must be the greatest prodi-
gality, since lost time is never found
again.
—Benjamin Franklin

THERE'S NEVER ENOUGH TIME

Curse ruthless time! Curse our mortality.
How cruelly short is the allotted span for
all we must cram into it!
—Sir Winston Churchill

There is a time for work. And a time for
love. That leaves no other time.
—Coco Chanel

Ah! the clock is always slow; it is later
than you think.
—Robert W. Service

The forty-four-hour week has no charm
for me. I'm looking for a forty-hour day.
—Nicholas Murray Butler

Those who make the worst use of their
time most complain of its brevity.
—Jean de La Bruyere

HAVING ENOUGH TIME

What we love to do we find time to do.
—John Lancaster Spalding

Time stays long enough for anyone who will use it.

—Anon.

It is nonsense to say there is not enough time to be fully informed.... Time given to thought is the greatest timesaver of all.
—Norman Cousins

There is time for everything.
—Thomas A. Edison

We shall never have more time. We have, and have always had, all the time there is. No object is served in waiting until next week or even until to-morrow. Keep going.... Concentrate on something useful.

—Arnold Bennett

We all find time to do what we really want to do.

—William Feather

Time is a fixed income and, as with any income, the real problem facing most of us is how to live successfully within our daily allotment.

—Margaret B. Johnstone

There is time enough for everything in the course of the day if you do but one thing at once; but there is not time enough in the year if you will do two things at a time.

—Lord Chesterfield

You will never "find" time for anything. If you want time you must make it.

—Charles Buxton

Make the most of today. Translate your good intentions into actual deeds.

—Grenville Kleiser

USING SMALL PIECES OF TIME

Much may be done in those little shreds
and patches of time which every day produces, and which most men throw away.
—Charles Caleb Colton

Learn to use ten minutes intelligently. It
will pay you huge dividends.
—William A. Irwin

It is better to do the most trifling thing
in the world than to regard half an hour
as trifle.
—Johann von Goethe

I recommend you to take care of the
minutes, for the hours will take care of
themselves.
—Lord Chesterfield

The butterfly counts not months but
moments, and has time enough.
—Rabindranath Tagore

The real secret of how to use time is to pack it as you would a portmanteau, filling up the small spaces with small things.
—Sir Henry Haddow

One must learn a different ... sense of time, one that depends more on small amounts than big ones.
—Sister Mary Paul

An earnest purpose finds time, or makes it. It seizes on spare moments, and turns fragments to golden account.
—William Ellery Channing

Guard well your spare moments. They are like uncut diamonds. Discard them and their value will never be known. Improve them and they will become the brightest gems in a useful life.
—Ralph Waldo Emerson

LIVING ONE DAY AT A TIME
IS A KEY TO HAPPINESS

That man is happiest who lives from day
to day and asks no more, garnering the
simple goodness of life.

—Euripides

Each day provides its own gifts.

—Martial

And that was victory. The freedom to
sprawl loosely upon a city street, heat his
coffee and eat a can of beans ... with no
enemy bullets forcing him to toss the can
aside while diving behind another wall
for momentary survival.

—David Douglas Duncan

The best way to secure future happiness
is to be as happy as is rightfully possible
today.

—Charles W. Eliot

It is only possible to live happily-ever-after on a day-to-day basis.
—Margaret Bonnano

Happiness is to be found along the way, not at the end of the road, for then the journey is over and it is too late. Today, this hour, this minute is the day, the hour, the minute for each of us to sense the fact that life is good, with all of its trials and troubles, and perhaps more interesting because of them.
—Robert R. Updegraff

Let us savour the swift delights of the most beautiful of our days!
—Alphonse de Lamartine

Death accompanies us at every step and enables us to use those moments when life smiles at us to feel more deeply the sweetness of life. The more certain the end, the more tempting the minute.
—Theodore Fontane

Happiness is produced not so much by great pieces of good fortune that seldom happen, as by little advantages that occur every day.

—Benjamin Franklin

To fill the hour, that is happiness; to fill the hour, and leave no crevice for a repentance or an approval.

—Ralph Waldo Emerson

My advice to you is not to inquire why or whither, but just to enjoy your ice cream while it's on your plate.

—Thornton Wilder

Those who face that which is actually before them, unburdened by the past, undistracted by the future, these are they who live, who make the best use of their lives; these are those who have found the secret of contentment.

—Alban Goodier

Live your life each day as you would climb a mountain. An occasional glance toward the summit keeps the goal in mind, but many beautiful scenes are to be observed from each new vantage point. Climb slowly, steadily, enjoying each passing moment; and the view from the summit will serve as a fitting climax for the journey.

—Harold B. Melchart

People who postpone happiness are like children who try chasing rainbows in an effort to find the pot of gold at the rainbow's end.... Your life will never be fulfilled until you are happy here and now.

—Ken Keyes, Jr.

If you are not happy here and now, you never will be.

—Taisen Deshimaru

Present joys are more to flesh and blood
Than the dull prospect of a distant good.

—John Dryden

Taking time to live is taking time to appreciate simple silence as better than any kind of talk, or watching a flower, or watching a guy wash the windows on a skyscraper and wondering what he is thinking.

—Gersi Douchan

In order to be utterly happy the only thing necessary is to refrain from comparing this moment with other moments in the past, which I often did not fully enjoy because I was comparing them with other moments of the future.

—André Gide

One day of pleasure is worth two of sorrow.

—Anon.

If you observe a really happy man, you will find ... that he is happy in the course of living life twenty-four crowded hours each day.

—W. Beran Wolfe

Happiness is not a state to arrive at, but a
manner of traveling.
                    —Margaret Lee Runback

Live in day-tight compartments.
                    —Dale Carnegie

He's one of those Christmas Eve guys.
There are people like that ... every day in
their lives is Christmas Eve.
                    —Joe Garagiola,
                    talking about Yogi Berri

Love, and do what you like.
                    —Saint Augustine

Happy the man, and happy he alone
He who can call today his own
He who, secure within, can say
"Tomorrow, do thy worst
For I have lived today."
                    —Henry Fielding

Some Basic Things to Do Each Day

There is no other solution to man's progress but the day's honest work, the day's honest decisions, the day's generous utterances and the day's good deed.

—Clare Boothe Luce

A man should hear a little music, read a little poetry, and see a fine picture every day of his life, in order that worldly cares may not obliterate the sense of the beautiful which God has implanted in the human soul.

—Johann von Goethe

I have resolved that from this day on, I will do all the business I can honestly, have all the fun I can reasonably, do all the good I can willingly, and save my digestion by thinking pleasantly.

—Robert Louis Stevenson

Today is the day in which to express your noblest qualities of mind and heart, to do at least one worthy thing which you have long postponed.

—Grenville Kleiser

Do what you can, with what you have, where you are.

—Theodore Roosevelt

Our grand business undoubtedly is not to see what lies dimly at a distance but to do what lies clearly at hand.

—Thomas Carlyle

My formula for living is quite simple. I get up in the morning and I go to bed at night. In between I occupy myself as best I can.

—Cary Grant

What you are afraid to do is a clear indicator of the next thing you need to do.

—Anon.

If we cannot meet our everyday sur-
roundings with equanimity and pleasure
and grow each day in some useful direction, then ... life is on the road toward
misfortune, misery and destruction.

—Luther Burbank

It isn't hard to be good from time to time
in sports. What's tough is being good
every day.

—Willie Mays

A day's work is a day's work, neither
more nor less, and the man who does it
needs a day's sustenance, a night's repose
and due leisure, whether he be painter or
ploughman.

—George Bernard Shaw

Make it a point to do something every
day that you don't want to do. This is the
golden rule for acquiring the habit of
doing your duty without pain.

—Mark Twain

A homer a day will boost my pay.
　　　　　　　　—Josh Gibson

Add each day something to fortify you
against poverty and death.
　　　　　　　　—Marcus Annaeus Seneca

Realize life as an end in itself.
Functioning is all there is.
　　　　　　　　—Oliver Wendell Holmes, Jr.

He has not learned the first lesson of life
who does not every day surmount a fear.
　　　　　　　　—Ralph Waldo Emerson

Act well at the moment, and you have
performed a good action to all eternity.
　　　　　　　　—Johann Kaspar Lavater

The great business of life is to be, to do,
to do without, and to depart.
　　　　　　　　—John, Viscount
　　　　　　　　Morley of Blackburn

If I had my life to live over, I would start barefoot earlier in the spring and stay that way later in the fall. I would go to more dances. I would ride more merry-go-rounds. I would pick more daisies.

—Nadine Stair

Nothing determines who we will become so much as those things we choose to ignore.

—Sandor Minab

Take the time to come home to yourself everyday.

—Robin Casarjean

The power of a man's virtue should not be measured by his special efforts, but by his ordinary doing.

—Blaise Pascal

Resolve to perform what you ought. Perform without fail what you resolve.

—Benjamin Franklin

Know what you want to do, hold the thought firmly, and do every day what should be done, and every sunset will see you that much nearer the goal.
—Elbert Hubbard

It is no easy thing for a principle to become a man's own unless each day he maintains it and works it out in his life.
—Epictetus

Showing up is 80 percent of life.
—Woody Allen

Resolve to edge in a little reading every day, if it is but a single sentence. If you gain fifteen minutes a day, it will make itself felt at the end of the year.
—Horace Mann

Each day can be one of triumph if you keep up your interests.
—George Matthew Adams

I work every day—or at least I force myself into my office or room. I may get nothing done, but you don't earn bonuses without putting in time. Nothing may come for three months, but you don't get the fourth without it.

—Mordecai Richler

When action grows unprofitable, gather information; when information grows unprofitable, sleep.

—Ursula K. LeGuin

Take short views, hope for the best, and trust in God.

—Sydney Smith

Do you know that disease and death must needs overtake us, no matter what we are doing?... What do you wish to be doing when it overtakes you? If you have anything better to be doing when you are so overtaken, get to work on that.

—Epictetus

I long to accomplish a great and noble task, but it is my chief duty to accomplish small tasks as if they were great and noble.

—Helen Keller

If you always do what interests you, at least one person is pleased.

—Katharine Hepburn's mother

To do the useful thing, to say the courageous thing, to contemplate the beautiful thing: that is enough for one man's life.

—T.S. Eliot

Have patience with all things, but chiefly have patience with yourself. Do not lose courage in considering your own imperfections, but instantly set about remedying them—every day begin the task anew.

—Saint Francis de Sales

Without duty, life is soft and boneless.

—Joseph Joubert

A man may fulfill the object of his existence by asking a question he cannot answer, and attempting a task he cannot achieve.

—Oliver Wendell Holmes

And each man stands with his face in the light of his own drawn sword. Ready to do what a hero can.

—Elizabeth Barrett Browning

Man goeth forth unto his work and to his labor until the evening.

—Ps. 104:23

Every day give yourself a good mental shampoo.

—Sara Jordan, M.D.

To look up and not down,
To look forward and not back,
To look out and not in, and
To lend a hand.

—Edward Everett Hale

Do all the good you can,
By all the means you can,
In all the ways you can,
In all the places you can,
At all the times you can.

—Anon.

I like the man who faces what he must,
With steps triumphant and a heart of
    cheer;
Who fights the daily battle without fear.
—Sarah Knowles Bolton

To accomplish our destiny ... [w]e must
cover before nightfall the distance
assigned to each of us.
—Dr. Alexis Carrel

Fulfill your works, your daily tasks.
—Ex. 5:13

Man goeth forth unto his work and to
his labor until the evening.
—Ps. 104:23

LIVING EACH DAY AS THOUGH IT WERE OUR LAST

He who would make serious use of his life must always act as though he had a long time to live and schedule his time as though he were about to die.

—Emile Littre

Each day should be passed as though it were our last.

—Publilius Syrus

To live each day as though one's last, never flustered, never apathetic, never attitudinizing—here is perfection of character.

—Marcus Aurelius

Every day is a little life ... live every day as if it would be the last. Those that dare lose a day are dangerously prodigal; those that dare misspend it are desperate.

—Joseph Hall

One should count each day a separate
life.

—Marcus Annaeus Seneca

Learn as if you were going to live forever. Live as if you were going to die
tomorrow.

—Anon.

You have to count on living every single
day in a way you believe will make you
feel good about your life—so that if it
were over tomorrow, you'd be content
with yourself.

—Jane Seymour

No one can confidently say that he will
still be living tomorrow.

—Euripides

Each day is a little life; every waking and
rising a little birth; every fresh morning a
little youth; every going to rest and sleep
a little death.

—Arthur Schopenhauer

DOING OUR BEST EVERY DAY

Do your best every day and your life will gradually expand into satisfying fullness.
—Horatio W. Dresser

Any man's life will be filled with constant and unexpected encouragement if he makes up his mind to do his level best each day.
—Booker T. Washington

Do each daily task the best we can; act as though the eye of opportunity were always upon us.
—William Feather

What a man accomplishes in a day depends upon the way in which he approaches his tasks. When we accept tough jobs as a challenge to our ability and wade into them with joy and enthusiasm, miracles can happen.
—Arland Gilbert

I still find each day too short for all the thoughts I want to think, all the walks I want to take, all the books I want to read, and all the friends I want to see.

—John Burroughs

So get a few laughs and do the best you can.

—Will Rogers

You may delay, but time will not.

—Benjamin Franklin

I come to the office each morning and stay for long hours doing what has to be done to the best of my ability. And when you've done the best you can, you can't do any better. So when I go to sleep I turn everything over to the Lord and forget it.

—Harry S. Truman

That man is blest who does his best and leaves the rest.

—Charles F. Deems

Do Something for Someone Else, Every Day

When you rise in the morning, form a
resolution to make the day a happy one
for a fellow creature.

—Sydney Smith

He who allows his day to pass by without
practicing generosity and enjoying life's
pleasures is like a blacksmith's bellows; he
breathes, but does not live.

—Sanskrit proverb

You have not lived a perfect day, even
though you have earned your money,
unless you have done something for someone who will never be able to repay you.

—Ruth Smeltzer

I expect to pass through life but once. If,
therefore, there can be any kindness I can
show, or any good thing I can do to any
fellow human being, let me do it now.

—William Penn

HAVE SOME FUN, SOME RELAXATION, EACH DAY

The most thoroughly wasted of all days
is that on which one has not laughed.
—Nicolas de Chamfort

Each day, and the living of it, has to be a
conscious creation in which discipline
and order are relieved with some play
and pure foolishness.

—May Sarton

The highest value in life is found in the
stewardship of time.
—Robert M. Fine

Friends, I beg you do not shirk your
daily task of indolence.

—Don Marquis

We should consider every day lost on
which we have not danced at least once.
—Friedrich Nietzsche

He who does not get fun and enjoyment
out of every day ... needs to reorganize
his life.

—George Matthew Adams

Unless each day can be looked back upon
by an individual as one in which he has
had some fun, some joy, some real satisfaction, that day is a loss.

—Anon.

Take time every day to do something
silly.

—Philipa Walker

I finally figured out the only reason to be
alive is to enjoy it.

—Rita Mae Brown

It's fun to get together and have something good to eat at least once a day.
That's what human life is all about—
enjoying things.

—Julia Child

Come, let us give a little time to folly ...
and even in a melancholy day let us find
time for an hour of pleasure.
                    —Saint Bonaventura

The value of life lies not in the length of
days, but in the use we make of them; a
man may live long yet live very little.
                    —Michel de Montaigne

No matter what looms ahead, if you can
eat today, enjoy the sunlight today, mix
good cheer with friends today, enjoy it
and bless God for it.
                    —Henry Ward Beecher

Have a time and place for everything,
and do everything in its time and place,
and you will not only accomplish more,
but have far more leisure than those who
are always hurrying.
                    —Tyron Edwards

BE SATISFIED WITH A
GOOD DAY'S WORK

There are hundreds of tasks we feel we must accomplish in the day, but if we do not take them one at a time ... we are bound to break our own physical or mental structure.

—Ted Bengermino

A man can do only what he can do. But if he does that each day he can sleep at night and do it again the next day.

—Albert Schweitzer

I come to the office each morning and stay for long hours doing what has to be done to the best of my ability. And when you've done the best you can, you can't do any better. So when I go to sleep I turn everything over to the Lord and forget it.

—Harry S. Truman

We cannot do everything at once, but we can do something at once.

—Calvin Coolidge

Always do one thing less than you think you can do.

—Bernard Baruch

Think that day lost whose descending sun, views from thy hand no noble action done.

—Joseph Joubert

Be ashamed to die until you have won some victory for humanity.

—Horace Mann

A day's work is a day's work, neither more nor less, and the man who does it needs a day's sustenance, a night's repose and due leisure, whether he be painter or ploughman.

—George Bernard Shaw

Sufficient to each day are the duties to be done and the trials to be endured.

—T.L. Gayler

If you want to kill time, try working it to death.

—Sam Levenson

I have fought a good fight, I have finished my course, I have kept the faith.

—2 Tm. 4:7

I look back on my life like a good day's work; it is done, and I am satisfied with it.

—Grandma Moses

Anyone can carry his burden, however hard, until nightfall. Anyone can do his work, however hard, for one day. Anyone can live sweetly, patiently, lovingly, purely, till the sun goes down. And this is all life really means.

—Robert Louis Stevenson

GOOD HABITS MAKE OUR DAILY LIVES EASIER

The moment we pass out of our habits we lose all sense of permanency and routine.

—George Moore

It is too bad if you have to do everything upon reflection and can't do anything from early habit.

—Georg Christoph Lichtenberg

Habits are safer than rules; you don't have to watch them. And you don't have to keep them, either; they keep you.

—Dr. Frank Crane

Most of life is routine—dull and grubby, but routine is the mountain that keeps a man going. If you wait for inspiration you'll be standing on the corner after the parade is a mile down the street.

—Ben Nicholas

Good habits, which bring our lower passions and appetites under automatic control, leave our natures free to explore the larger experiences of life.
—Ralph W. Sockman, D.D.

Motivation is what gets you started. Habit is what keeps you going.
—Jim Ryuh

Without the aid of prejudice and custom, I should not be able to find my way across the room.
—William Hazlitt

Habit is not mere subjugation, it is a tender tie; when one remembers habit it seems to have been happiness.
—Elizabeth Bowen

To learn new habits is everything, for it is to reach the substance of life. Life is but a tissue of habits.
—Henri Frederic Amiel

Choose always the way that seems the best, however rough it may be; custom will soon render it easy and agreeable.
—Pythagoras

Quality is not an act. It is a habit.
—Aristotle

It is not in novelty but in habit that we find the greatest pleasure.
—Raymond Radiguet

Habit is stronger than reason.
—George Santayana

Character is simply habit long enough continued.
—Plutarch

Nothing is more powerful than habit.
—Ovid

SOMETIMES, THE BEST WE CAN DO IS JUST MAKE IT THROUGH THE DAY

Come what may, time and the hour runs through the roughest day.
—William Shakespeare

At any rate, you can bear it for a quarter of an hour!
—Theodore Haecker

The longest day is soon ended.
—Pliny, the Younger

The secret of my success is that I always managed to live to fly another day.
—Chuck Yeager

If you do the same thing every day at the same time for the same length of time, you'll save yourself from many a sink. Routine is a condition of survival.
—Flannery O'Connor

How Long Is a Day?

A day is a miniature eternity.
> —Ralph Waldo Emerson

A day is a span of time no one is wealthy
enough to waste.
> —Anon.

One day, with life and heart, is more
than time enough to find a world.
> —James Russell Lowell

The time which we have at our disposal
every day is elastic; the passions that we
feel expand it, those that we inspire contract it; and habit fills up what remains.
> —Marcel Proust

Every day is a messenger of God.
> —Russian proverb

TIME IS RELATIVE

When a man sits with a pretty girl for an hour, it seems like a minute. But let him sit on a hot stove for a minute, and it's longer than any hour. That's relativity.

—Albert Einstein

Time is
Too slow for those who wait,
Too swift for those who fear,
Too long for those who grieve,
Too short for those who rejoice.
But for those who love, time is not.

—Henry van Dyke

The less one has to do, the less time one finds to do it in. One yawns, one procrastinates, one can do it when one will, and, therefore, one seldom does it at all; whereas those who have a great deal of business must buckle to it; and then they always find time enough to do it.

—Lord Chesterfield

Time is nothing absolute; its duration depends on the rate of thought and feeling.

—John Draper

Time is a fluid condition which has no existence except in the momentary avatars of individual people.

—William Faulkner

What then is time? If no one asks me, I know what it is. If I wish to explain it to him who asks, I do not know.

—Saint Augustine

Time is the product of changing realities, beings, existences.

—Nicholas Berdyaev

Time is the relationship between events.

—Yakima Indian Nation

Time is the arbitrary division of eternity.

—Anon.

Time is a part of eternity, and of the same piece with it.
>—Moses Mendelssohn

Time is eternity begun.
>—James Montgomery

Time is not a line, but a series of now-points.
>—Taisen Deshimaru

You can't measure time in days the way you can money in dollars, because each day is different.
>—Phillip Hewett

An hour of pain is as long as a day of pleasure.
>—Anon.

Reality is a staircase going neither up nor down, we don't move; today is today, always is today.
>—Octavio Paz

OTHER DEFINITIONS OF TIME

What runs through a person like water
through a sieve.

—Samuel Butler

Scrolls: write on them what you want to
be remembered for.

—Joseph Ibn Pakuda

Time is an avid gambler who has no
need to cheat to win every time.

—Charles Baudelaire

Time is the only critic without ambition.

—John Steinbeck

Time is the most valuable thing a man
can spend.

—Theophrastus

Time is a storm in which we are all lost.

—William C. Williams

63

Time is the tyrant of the body.
                                    —Anon.

Time is the wisest counsellor of all.
                                    —Pericles

Time is the moving image of eternity.
                                    —Plato

Time is the soul of this world.
                                    —Plutarch

Time is a sandpile we run our fingers in.
                                    —Carl Sandburg

Time is one kind of robber whom the
law does not strike at, and who steals
what is most precious to men.
                                    —Napoleon Bonaparte

Time is that in which all things pass
away.
                                    —Arthur Schopenhauer

Time is a file that wears and makes no noise.

> —English proverb

Time is what we want most, but ... what we use worst.

> —William Penn

Time is the king of men.

> —William Shakespeare

Time is the dressing room for eternity.

> —Anon.

Time itself is an element.

> —Johann von Goethe

Time is the devourer of all things.

> —Ovid

Time is a very shadow that passeth away.

> —Apocrypha

Time is the subtle thief of youth.

> —John Milton

Time is a wealth of change, but the clock
in its parody makes it mere change and
no wealth.

—Rabindranath Tagore

Time is the rider that breaks youth.

—George Herbert

Time is an eternal guest that banquets on
our ideals and bodies.

—Elbert Hubbard

The surest poison is time.

—Ralph Waldo Emerson

Time is a great manager: it arranges
things well.

—Pierre Corneille

Time is the greatest and longest-estab-
lished spinner of all.... His factory is a
secret place, his work noiseless, and his
hands are mutes.

—Charles Dickens

Time is the stuff life's made of.
> —David Belasco

Time is an illusion—to orators.
> —Elbert Hubbard

Time is the silent, never-resting thing ... rolling, rushing on, swift, silent, like an all-embracing oceantide, on which we and all the universe swim.
> —Thomas Carlyle

Time is my estate: to Time I'm heir.
> —Johann von Goethe

Time is change, transformation, evolution.
> —Isaac L. Peretz

Time is a circus always packing up and moving away.
> —Ben Hecht

Time is but the stream I go a-fishing in.
> —Henry David Thoreau

Time is a river without banks.
                              —Marc Chagall

Time is a flowing river. Happy those who allow themselves to be carried, unresisting, with the current. They float through easy days. They live, unquestioning, in the moment.
                              —Christopher Morley

Time is the greatest innovator.
                              —Francis Bacon

Time is a dressmaker specializing in alterations.
                              —Faith Baldwin

Time is the author of authors.
                              —Francis Bacon

Time is a stream which glides smoothly on and is past before we know.
                              —Ovid

PART TWO

YESTERDAY: THE PAST

WE REMEMBER MORE
OF THE GOOD THAN OF THE BAD
OR THE DIFFICULT

Vanity plays lurid tricks with our memory.
—Joseph Conrad

Nostalgia is a seductive liar.
—George W. Ball

Nostalgia: A device that removes the ruts
and potholes from memory lane.
—Doug Larson

What was hard to bear is sweet to
remember.
—Portuguese proverb

The heart's memory eliminates the bad
and magnifies the good; and thanks to
this artifice we manage to endure the
burdens of the past.
—Gabriel Garcia Marquez

70

A man's memory may almost become the art of continually varying and misrepresenting his past, according to his interest in the present.

—George Santayana

Praising what is lost makes the remembrance dear.

—William Shakespeare

Some folks never exaggerate—they just remember big.

—Audrey Snead

God gave us memory that we might have roses in December.

—Sir James M. Barrie

They say you should not suffer through the past. You should be able to wear it like a loose garment, take it off and let it drop.

—Eva Jessye

People Have Always thought "The Good Old Days" Were Better

Children today are tyrants. They contradict their parents, gobble their food, and tyrannize their teachers.
>—Socrates (470–399 B.C.)

Only sick music makes money today.
>—Friedrich Nietzsche (in 1888)

There has never been an age that did not applaud the past and lament the present.
>—Lillian Eichler Watson

Let others praise ancient times; I am glad I was born in these.
>—Ovid (81 B.C.)

Posterity will say as usual: "In the past things were better, the present is worse than the past."
>—Anton Chekhov (1860–1904)

Our ignorance of history makes us libel to our own times. People have always been like this.

—Gustave Flaubert (1821–1880)

Oh, this age! How tasteless and ill-bred it is!

—Catullus (87–54 B.C.)

This strange disease of modern life, with its sick hurry, its divided aims.

—Matthew Arnold (1822–1888)

The illusion that times that were are better than those that are has probably pervaded all ages.

—Horace Greeley (1811–1872)

The "good old times"—all times, when old, are good.

—Lord Byron (1788–1824)

Oh, what times! Oh, what standards!

—Cicero (106–43 B.C.)

Probably no one alive hasn't at one time or another brooded over the possibility of going back to an earlier, ideal age in his existence and living a different kind of life.

—Hal Boyle

There is no greater sorrow than to recall a happy time in the midst of wretchedness.

—Dante Alighieri

The Golden Age was never the present Age.

—Thomas Fuller (1608–1661)

The worst time is always the present.

—Jean de La Fontaine (1621–1695)

Our ignorance of history makes us libel our own times. People have always been like this.

—Gustave Flaubert

REGRETS

If you have behaved badly, repent, make what amends you can and address yourself to the task of behaving better next time. On no account brood over your wrongdoing. Rolling in the muck is not the best way of getting clean.

—Aldous Huxley

When one door closes another opens. But we often look so long and so regretfully upon the closed door that we fail to see the one that has opened for us.

—Alexander Graham Bell

Regret for the things we did can be tempered by time; it is regret for the things we did not do that is inconsolable.

—Sydney J. Harris

Always repenting of wrongs done will never bring my heart to rest.

—Chi K'ang

The error of the past is the success of the future. A mistake is evidence that some-one tried to do something.

—Anon.

Regret is an appalling waste of energy; you can't build on it; it is good only for wallowing.

—Katherine Mansfield

I have always found that each step we take in life is to be regretted—if we once begin to wonder how many other steps might have been possible.

—John Oliver Hobbes

Let the dead Past bury its dead!
—Henry Wadsworth Longfellow

"The horror of that moment," the King went on, "I shall never forget." "You will, though," the Queen said, "if you don't make a memorandum of it."

—Lewis Carroll

Reflect upon your present blessings, of which every man has many—not on your past misfortunes, of which all men have some.

—Charles Dickens

If you cannot get rid of the family skeleton, you may as well make it dance.

—George Bernard Shaw

Hindsight is always 20/20.

—Billy Wilder

This is another day! Are its eyes blurred with maudlin grief for any wasted past? A thousand thousand failures shall not daunt! Let dust clasp dust, death, death; I am alive!

—Don Marquis

Your past is always going to be the way it was. Stop trying to change it.

—Anon.

We should have no regrets.... The past is finished. There is nothing to be gained by going over it. Whatever it gave us in the experiences it brought us was something we had to know.

—Rebecca Beard

The only thing I regret about my past is the length of it. If I had to live my life again, I'd make the same mistakes, only sooner.

—Tallulah Bankhead

Yesterday's errors let yesterday cover.

—Susan Coolidge

Whatever with the past has gone, the best is always yet to come.

—Lucy Larcom

We crucify ourselves between two thieves: regret for yesterday and fear of tomorrow.

—Fulton Oursler

LEARNING FROM THE PAST

Recognizing what we have done in the past is a recognition of ourselves. By conducting a dialogue with our past, we are searching how to go forward.

—Kiyoko Takeda

I know of no way of judging the future but by the past.

—Patrick Henry

Those who cannot remember the past are condemned to repeat it.

—George Santayana

The past is never dead—it is not even past.

—William Faulkner

The past is the best way to suppose what may come.

—Lord Halifax

Past: Our cradle, not our prison, and there is danger as well as appeal in its glamour. The past is for inspiration, not imitation; for continuation, not repetition.

—Israel Zangwill

Life can only be understood backwards, but it must be lived forward.

—Søren Kierkegaard

When I want to understand what is happening today or try to decide what will happen tomorrow, I look back.

—Oliver Wendell Holmes

We live in the present, we dream of the future, but we learn eternal truths from the past.

—Madame Chiang Kai-shek

The past is the best prophet of the future.

—Lord Byron

The past will not tell us what we ought to do, but ... what we ought to avoid.
—José Ortega y Gasset

Tomorrow hopes we have learned something from yesterday.
—John Wayne

Judgement comes from experience, and great judgement comes from bad experience.
—Robert Packwood

The only use of a knowledge of the past is to equip us for the present.
—Alfred North Whitehead

When the past has taught us that we have more within us than we have ever used, our prayer is a cry to the divine to come to us and fill us with its power.
—Rudolph Steiner

It's Important to Bury the Past, to Let It Go—to Move On

Here lies my past,
Goodbye I have kissed it;
Thank you kids,
I wouldn't have missed it.

—Ogden Nash

One must never lose time in vainly
regretting the past or in complaining
against the changes which cause us dis-
comfort, for change is the essence of life.

—Anatole France

Living in the past is a dull and lonely
business; looking back strains the neck
muscles, causes you to bump into people
not going your way.

—Edna Ferber

I demolish my bridges behind me ... then
there is no choice but forward.

—Firdtjof Nansen

Let the past drift away with the water.

             —Japanese proverb

Not the power to remember, but its very opposite, the power to forget, is a necessary condition for our existence.

             —Sholem Asch

You cannot step twice into the same river, for other waters are continually flowing on.

             —Heraclitus

Better by far you should forget and smile, than that you should remember and be sad.

             —Christina Rosetti

The past should be culled like a box of fresh strawberries, rinsed of debris, sweetened judiciously and served in small portions, not very often.

             —Laura Palmer

May I forget what ought to be forgotten;
and recall, unfailing, all that ought to be
recalled, each kindly thing, forgetting
what might sting.
        —Maty Caroline Davies

Here's to the past. Thank God it's past!
        —Anon.

One must be thrust out of a finished
cycle in life, and that leap is the most difficult to make—to part with one's faith,
one's love, when one would prefer to
renew the faith and recreate the passion.
        —Anaïs Nin

The biggest thing in today's sorrow is the
memory of yesterday's joy.
        —Kahlil Gibran

The worst thing you can do is to try to
cling to something that's gone, or to
recreate it.
        —Johnette Napolitano

Ne'er look for the birds of this year in the nests of the last.

> —Miguel de Cervantes

Don't look back. Something may be gaining on you.

> —Satchel Paige

The dogmas of the quiet past are inadequate to the stormy present.

> —Abraham Lincoln

Anyone who limits her vision to memories of yesterday is already dead.

> —Lily Langtry

I like the dreams for the future better than the history of the past.

> —Thomas Jefferson

The first recipe for happiness is: Avoid too lengthy meditations on the past.

> —André Maurois

The past is a funeral gone by.
—Edmund Gosse

How the past perishes is how the future
becomes.
—Alfred North Whitehead

Never let yesterday use up today.
—Richard H. Nelson

The past is a guidepost, not a hitching
post.
—L. Thomas Holdcroft

That sign of old age, extolling the past at
the expense of the present.
—Sydney Smith

The best compliment we can pay our
past is to prophetically and bravely face
today and tomorrow.
—Bernie Wiebe

THE PAST AS PROLOGUE—
A BEGINNING

The past is but the beginning of a beginning, and all that is and has been is but
the twilight of the dawn.

> —H. G. Wells

Nor deem the irrevocable Past
As wholly wasted, wholly vain,
If, rising on its wrecks, at last
To something nobler we attain.

> —Henry Wadsworth Longfellow

The good old days were never that good,
believe me. The good new days are today,
and better days are coming tomorrow.
Our greatest songs are still unsung.

> —Hubert H. Humphrey

Nothing is predestined: The obstacles of
your past can become the gateways that
lead to new beginnings.

> —Ralph Blum

What's past is prologue.
> —William Shakespeare

Visualize yourself standing before a gateway on a hilltop. Your entire life lies out before you and below. Before you step through, pause and review the past; the learning and the joys, the victories and the sorrows—everything it took to bring you here.
> —*The Book of Runes*

The past is never completely lost, however extensive the devastation. Your sorrows are the bricks and mortar of a magnificent temple. What you are today and what you will be tomorrow are because of what you have been.
> —Gordon Wright

We have to do with the past only as we can make it useful to the present and the future.
> —Frederick Douglass

YESTERDAY AND TOMORROW

Fear not for the future, weep not for the past.

> —Percy Bysshe Shelley

There are two days about which nobody should ever worry, and these are yesterday and tomorrow.

> —Robert Jones Burdette

Every saint has a past, and every sinner has a future.

> —Oscar Wilde

No yesterdays are ever wasted for those who give themselves to today.

> —Brendan Francis

Yesterday I lived, today I suffer, tomorrow I die; but I still think fondly, today and tomorrow, of yesterday.

> —Gotthold Ephraim Lessing

MANY THINGS REMAIN THE SAME

I'm not convinced that the world is in any worse shape than it ever was. It's just that in this age of almost instantaneous communication, we bear the weight of problems our forefathers only read about after they were solved.

—Burton Hillis

The world's history is constant, like the laws of nature, and simple, like the souls of men.

—J.C.F. von Schiller

This time, like all times, is a very good one if we but know what to do with it.

—Ralph Waldo Emerson

In times like these, it helps to recall that there have always been times like these.

—Paul Harvey

GENERAL QUOTATIONS ABOUT THE PAST

Respect the past in the full measure of its deserts, but do not make the mistake of confusing it with the present, nor seek in it the ideals of the future.

—José Ingenieros

The past in retrospect holds manifold disenchantments, failures and even tragedies; and yet the worse may be forgotten and the best held fast.

—W. Robertson Neicoll

The past is a work of art, free of irrelevancies and loose ends.

—Max Beerbohm

When I am anxious it is because I am living in the future. When I am depressed it is because I am living in the past.

—Anon.

Each has his past shut in him like the leaves of a book shown to him by heart, and his friends can only read the title.

—Virginia Woolf

The good old days are neither better nor worse than the ones we're living through right now.

—Artie Shaw

We are well advised to keep on nodding terms with the people we used to be, whether we find them attractive company or not.... We forget all too soon the things we thought we could never forget.

—Joan Didion

The past is a foreign country; they do things differently there.

—Leslie Poles Hartley

The past is the tomorrow that got away.

—Leonard L. Levinson

The past with its pleasures, its rewards,
its foolishness, its punishments, is there
for each of us forever, and it should be.
                              —Lillian Hellman

Our deeds still travel with us from afar,
and what we have been makes us what
we are.
                              —George Eliot

No past is dead for us, but only sleeping,
love.
                              —Helen Hunt Jackson

Why should we grope among the dry
bones of the past, or put the living gen-
eration into masquerade out of its faded
wardrobe?
                              —Ralph Waldo Emerson

The past not merely is not fugitive, it
remains present.
                              —Marcel Proust

Of all sad words of tongue or pen, the
saddest are these: It might have been.
—John Greenleaf Whittier

The past is that which we possess fully
and in whole.
—Isidor Eliashev

Our life is like some vast lake that is
slowly filling with the stream of our
years. As the waters creep surely upward
the landmarks of the past are one by one
submerged. But there shall always be
memory to lift its head above the tide
until the lake is overflowing.
—Alexandre Charles Auguste Bisson

The past is one evil less and one memory
more.
—Elbert Hubbard

Then is then. Now is now. We must
grow to learn the difference.
—Anon.

Say not thou, what is the cause that the former days were better than these, for thou dost not inquire wisely concerning this.

—Eccl. 7:10

The past which is so presumptuously brought forward as a precedent for the present was itself founded on some past that went before it.

—Madame de Stael

"Old times" never come back and I suppose it's just as well. What comes back is a new morning every day in the year, and that's better.

—George E. Woodberry

Life in the twentieth century undeniably has ... such richness, joy and adventure as were unknown to our ancestors except in their dreams.

—Arthur H. Campton

We have inherited new difficulties because we have inherited more privileges.

—Dr. Abram Sacher

People are always asking about the good old days. I say, why don't you say the good "now" days? Isn't "now" the only time you're living?

—Robert M. Young

Enjoy yourself. These are the "good old days" you're going to miss in the years ahead.

—Anon.

The past is our very being.

—David Ben-Gurion

To disdain today is to prove that yesterday has been misunderstood.

—Maurice Maeterlinck

PART THREE

TODAY: THE PRESENT

THE IMPORTANCE OF TODAY

This is not a dress rehearsal. This is It.
>   —Tom Cunningham

Seize the day, and put the least possible
trust in tomorrow.
>   —Horace

Tomorrow's life is too late. Live today.
>   —Martial

One today is worth two tomorrows.
>   —Benjamin Franklin

Half of today is better than all of tomorrow.
>   —Jean de La Fontaine

Never put off until tomorrow what you
can do today, because if you enjoy it
today, you can do it again, tomorrow.
>   —Anon.

The present moment is significant, not as the bridge between past and future, but by reason of its contents, which can fill our emptiness and become ours, if we are capable of receiving them.

—Dag Hammarskjold

Now is the only time we own; give, love, toil with a will.
And place no faith in tomorrow, for the clock may then be still.

—Anon.

Today is the first day of the rest of your life.

—Abbie Hoffman

All of us tend to put off living. We are all dreaming of some magical rose garden over the horizon instead of enjoying the roses that are blooming outside our windows today.

—Dale Carnegie

It's not that "today is the first day of the rest of my life," but that now is all there is of my life.

—Hugh Prather

You had better live your best and act your best and think your best today; for today is the sure preparation for tomorrow and all the other tomorrows that follow.

—Harriet Martineau

We want to live in the present, and the only history that is worth a tinker's damn is the history we make today.

—Henry Ford

Happy the man, and happy he alone
He can call today his own.
He who, secure within can say,
"Tomorrow, do thy worst, for I have
    lived today."

—Henry Fielding

So often we rob tomorrow's memories by today's economies.

—John Mason Brown

Enjoy yourself, drink, call the life you live today your own—but only that; the rest belongs to chance.

—Euripides

You are younger today than you ever will be again. Make use of it for the sake of tomorrow.

—Anon.

If we are ever to enjoy life, now is the time, not tomorrow or next year.... Today should always be our most wonderful day.

—Thomas Dreier

Live now, believe me, wait not till tomorrow, gather the roses of life today.

—Pierre de Ronsard

Forget mistakes. Forget failures. Forget everything except what you're going to do now and do it. Today is your lucky day.

—Will Durant

He growled at morning, noon, and
     night,
And trouble sought to borrow;
Although today the sky was bright,
He knew t'would storm tomorrow;
A thought of joy he could not stand,
And struggled to resist it;
Though sunshine dappled all the land
This sorry pessimist it.

—Nixon Waterman

Yesterday is ashes; tomorrow wood.
Only today does the fire burn brightly.
     —Old Eskimo proverb

One of these days is none of these days.
     —H.G. Bohn

In the present, every day is a miracle.
> —James Gould Cozzens

Look lovingly upon the present, for it
holds the only things that are forever
true.
> —*A Course In Miracles*

This is the day which the Lord has made.
Let us rejoice and be glad in it.
> —Ps. 118:24

To those leaning on the sustaining infinite, to-day is big with blessings.
> —Mary Baker Eddy

The here-and-now is no mere filling of
time, but a filling of time with God.
> —John Foster

Life is only this place, this time, and
these people right here and now.
> —Vincent Collins

I believe that only one person in a thousand knows the trick of really living in the present.

—Storm Jameson

There is one thing we can do, and the happiest people are those who do it to the limit of their ability. We can be completely present. We can be all here. We can ... give all our attention to the opportunity before us.

—Mark Van Doren

The future belongs to those who live intensely in the present.

—Anon.

The more I give myself permission to live in the moment and enjoy it without feeling guilty or judgmental about any other time, the better I feel about the quality of my work.

—Wayne Dyer

Act—act in the living Present!
>—Henry Wadsworth Longfellow

Are not my days few? Cease then, and let me alone, that I may take comfort a little, Before I go to the place from which I shall not return.
>—Jb. 10:21–22

Now or never was the time.
>—Laurence Sterne

And now, Lord, what wait I for?
>—Psalms

The present is elastic to embrace infinity.
>—Louis Anspacher

The present is the living sum-total of the whole past.
>—Thomas Carlyle

The present is an eternal now.
>—Abraham Cowley

One realm we have never conquered: the pure present.

—D.H. Lawrence

He who lives in the present lives in eternity.

—Ludwig Wittgenstein

The present is all the ready money Fate can give.

—Abraham Cowley

The present is an edifice which God cannot rebuild.

—Ralph Waldo Emerson

The present is the blocks with which we build.

—Henry Wadsworth Longfellow

The present is the symbol and vehicle of the future.

—Joseph McSorely

The present is all you have for your certain possession.

—Anon.

Having spent the better part of my life trying either to relive the past or experience the future before it arrives, I have come to believe that in between these two extremes is peace.

—Anon.

This time, like all times, is a very good one if we but know what to do with it.
—Ralph Waldo Emerson

The time is always right to do what is right.

—Martin Luther King, Jr.

I am in the present. I cannot know what tomorrow will bring forth. I can know only what the truth is for me today. That is what I am called upon to serve.

—Igor Stravinsky

The present offers itself to our touch for only an instant of time and then eludes the senses.

—Plutarch

We are here and it is now. Further than that, all knowledge is moonshine.

—H.L. Mencken

A life uncommanded now is uncommanded; a life unenjoyed now is unenjoyed; a life not lived wisely now is not lived wisely.

—David Grayson

The word "now" is like a bomb thrown through the window, and it ticks.

—Arthur Miller

Whether it's the best of times or the worst of times, it's the only time we've got.

—Art Buchwald

It is now, and in this world, that we must live.

—André Gide

Who cares about great marks left behind? We have one life ... Just one. Our life. We have nothing else.

—Ugo Betti

This—the immediate, everyday, and present experience—is IT, the entire and ultimate point for the existence of a universe.

—Alan Watts

Work accomplished means little. It is in the past. What we all want is the glorious and living present.

—Sherwood Anderson

Yesterday is a cancelled check. Tomorrow is a promissory note. Today is cash in hand. Spend It!

—John W. Newbern

TODAY RELATIVE TO YESTERDAY AND TOMORROW

Yesterday is but a dream, tomorrow is only a vision. But today, well lived, makes every yesterday a dream of happiness, and every tomorrow a vision of hope. Look well, therefore, to this day, for it is life, the very life of life.

—The Sanskrit

Do not look back on happiness, or dream of it in the future. You are only sure of today; do not let yourself be cheated out of it.

—Henry Ward Beecher

I am not afraid of tomorrow, for I have seen yesterday and I love today.

—William Allen White

The past, the present and the future are really one: they are today.

—Harriet Beecher Stowe

The present contains all that there is. It is holy ground; for it is the past, and it is the future.

> —Alfred North Whitehead

With the past, I have nothing to do; nor with the future. I live now.

> —Ralph Waldo Emerson

Children have neither a past nor a future. Thus they enjoy the present, which seldom happens to us.

> —Jean de La Bruyere

The past is a bucket of ashes, so live not in your yesterdays, nor just for tomorrow, but in the here and now.

> —Carl Sandburg

Everyman's life lies within the present, for the past is spent and done with, and the future is uncertain.

> —Marcus Aurelius

No mind is much employed upon the present; recollection and anticipation fill up almost all our moments.

—Samuel Johnson

It is not the weight of the future or the past that is pressing upon you, but ever that of the present alone. Even this burden, too, can be lessened if you confine it strictly to its own limits.

—Marcus Aurelius

We can easily manage if we will only take, each day, the burden appointed to it. But the load will be too heavy for us if we carry yesterday's burden over again today, and then add the burden of the morrow before we are required to bear it.

—John Newton

Past, and to come, seems best; things present, worst.

—William Shakespeare

Take in the ideas of the day, drain off those of yesterday. As to the morrow, time enough to consider it when it becomes today.

—Edward Bulwer-Lytton

Tomorrow I will live, the fool does say; today itself's too late, the wise lived yesterday.

—Martial

The cares of today are seldom those of tomorrow.

—William Cowper

Yesterday is a cancelled check; tomorrow is a promissory note; today is the only cash you have—so spend it wisely.

—Kay Lyons

The flesh endures the storms of the present alone, the mind those of the past and future as well.

—Epicurus

I try to learn from the past, but I plan for the future by focusing exclusively on the present. That's where the fun is.

—Donald Trump

The only living life is in the past and future—the present is an interlude—strange interlude in which we call on past and future to bear witness that we are living.

—Eugene O'Neill

The past cannot be regained, although we can learn from it; the future is not yet ours even though we must plan for it.... Time is now. We have only today.

—Charles Hummell

Look not mournfully into the past, it comes not back again. Wisely improve the present, it is thine. Go forth to meet the shadowy future without fear and with a manly heart.

—Henry Wadsworth Longfellow

No longer forward nor behind I look in hope or fear; but grateful, take the good I find, the best of now and here.
—John Greenleaf Whittier

The present, like a note in music, is nothing but as it appertains to what is past and what is to come.
—Walter Savage Landor

We can see well into the past; we can guess shrewdly in to the future; but that which is rolled up and muffled in impenetrable folds is today.
—Ralph Waldo Emerson

Patterns of the past echo in the present and resound through the future.
—Dhyani Ywahoo

It is difficult to live in the present, ridiculous to live in the future and impossible to live in the past.
—Jim Bishop

The present time is seldom able to fill desire or imagination with immediate enjoyment, and we are forced to supply its deficiencies by recollection or anticipation.

—Samuel Johnson

If we spend our time with regrets over yesterday, and worries over what might happen tomorrow, we have no today in which to live.

—Anon.

Now is all we have. Everything that has ever happened to you, and anything that is ever going to happen to you, is just a thought.

—Wayne Dyer

If you have one eye on yesterday, and one eye on tomorrow, you're going to be cockeyed today.

—Anon.

Yesterday has gone. Tomorrow may never come. There is only the miracle of this moment. Savor it. It is a gift.

—Anon.

When we have a world of only now, with no shadows of yesterdays or clouds of tomorrow, then saying what we can do will work.

—Goldie Ivener

The present is the now, the here, through which all future plunges to the past.

—James Joyce

I just take one day. Yesterday is gone. Tomorrow has not come. We have only today to love Jesus.

—Mother Teresa

Who controls the past controls the future; who controls the present controls the past.

—George Orwell

The idea of "twenty-four-hour living" applies primarily to the emotional life of the individual. Emotionally speaking, we must not live in yesterday, nor in tomorrow.

—*As Bill Sees It*

The present is the necessary product of all the past, the necessary cause of all the future.

—Robert G. Ingersoll

I can feel guilty about the past, apprehensive about the future, but only in the present can I act. The ability to be in the present moment is a major component of mental wellness.

—Abraham Maslow

If we open a quarrel between the past and the present, we shall find we have lost the future.

—Sir Winston Churchill

Few of us ever live in the present, we are forever anticipating what is to come or remembering what has gone.

—Louis L'Amour

Today is yesterday's effect and tomorrow's cause.

—Phillip Gribble

The secret of health for both mind and body is not to mourn for the past, not to worry about the future, nor to anticipate troubles, but to live the present moment wisely and earnestly.

—Buddha

I have realized that the past and the future are real illusions, that they exist only in the present, which is what there is and all that there is.

—Alan Watts

Today is yesterday's pupil.

—Benjamin Franklin

There is no present or future, only the past, happening over and over again, now.

—Eugene O'Neill

Don't waste today regretting yesterday instead of making a memory for tomorrow.

—Laura Palmer

Today was once the future from which you expected so much in the past.

—Anon.

Through loyalty to the past, our mind refuses to realize that tomorrow's joy is possible only if today's makes way for it; that each wave owes the beauty of its line only to the withdrawal of the preceding one.

—André Gide

Today is the blocks with which we build.

—Henry Wadsworth Longfellow

I have everything I need to enjoy my here and now—unless I am letting my consciousness be dominated by demands and expectations based on the dead past or the imagined future.

—Ken Keyes, Jr.

In order to be utterly happy, the only thing necessary is to refrain from comparing this moment with other moments in the past, which I often did not fully enjoy because I was comparing them with other moments of the future.

—André Gide

Very few men, properly speaking, live at present, but are providing to live another time.

—Jonathan Swift

Study as if you were to live forever. Live as if you were to die tomorrow.

—Isidore of Seville

Don't Waste Today Preparing for Tomorrow

Seize from every moment its unique novelty, and do not prepare your joys.
—André Gide

Do not manage as if you had ten thousand years before you. Look you, death stands at your elbow; make the most of your minute, and be good for something while it is in your power.
—Charles Palmer

As we are always preparing to be happy, it is inevitable that we should never be so.
—Blaise Pascal

Why not seize the pleasure at once? How often is happiness destroyed by preparation, foolish preparation!
—Jane Austen

When shall we live if not now?

　　　　　　　　—M.F.K. Fisher

Let us live today.

　　　　　　　—J.C.F. von Schiller

We cannot put off living until we are ready. The most salient characteristic of life is its coerciveness: it is always urgent, "here and now," without any possible postponement. Life is fired at us point-blank.

　　　　　　　—José Ortega y Gasset

Real generosity toward the future lies in giving all to the present.

　　　　　　　—Albert Camus

The greater part of our lives is spent in dreaming over the morrow, and when it comes, it, too, is consumed in the anticipation of a brighter morrow, and so the cheat is prolonged, even to the grave.

　　　　　　　—Mark Rutherford

Freedom from worries and surcease
from strain are illusions that always
inhabit the distance.

—Edwin Way Teale

The best preparation for a better life next
year is a full, complete, harmonious, joy-
ous life this year.

—Thomas Dreier

If you spend your whole life waiting for
the storm, you'll never enjoy the sunshine.

—Morris West

Some people are making such thorough
preparation for rainy days that they aren't
enjoying today's sunshine.

—William Feather

It is cheap generosity which promises the
future in compensation for the present.

—J.A. Spender

Who knows if the gods above will add
tomorrow's span to this day's sum?
—Horace

The most effective way to ensure the
value of the future is to confront the present courageously and constructively.
—Rollo May

Defer not till tomorrow to be wise,
tomorrow's sun to thee may never rise.
—William Congreve

My head is buried in the sands of tomorrow, while my tail feathers are singed by
the hot sun of today.
—John Barrymore

You do well to have visions of a better
life than of every day, but it is the life of
every day from which the elements of a
better life must come.
—Maurice Maeterlinck

Life wastes itself while we are preparing
to live.
—Ralph Waldo Emerson

Men spend their lives in anticipation, in
determining to be vastly happy at some
period when they have time. But the present time has one advantage over every
other—it is our own.... We may lay in a
stock of pleasures, as we would lay in a
stock of wine; but if we defer the tasting
of them too long, we shall find that both
are soured by age.
—Charles Caleb Colton

I have always been waiting for something
better—sometimes to see the best I had
snatched from me.
—Dorothy Reed Mendenhall

Today, well lived, will prepare me for
both the pleasure and the pain of
tomorrow.
—Anon.

Every moment that I am centered in the future, I suffer a temporary loss of this life.

—Hugh Prather

The future belongs to those who live intensely in the present.

—Anon.

We know nothing of tomorrow; our business is to be good and happy today.

—Sydney Smith

We are always beginning to live, but are never living.

—Manilius

The habit of looking into the future and thinking that the whole meaning of the present lies in what it will bring forth is a pernicious one. There can be no value in the whole unless there is value in the parts.

—Bertrand Russell

Very strange is this quality of our human nature which decrees that unless we feel a future before us we do not live completely in the present.

—Phillips Brooks

You don't save a pitcher for tomorrow. Tomorrow it may rain.

—Leo Durocher

Just do your best today and tomorrow will come ... tomorrow's going to be a busy day, a happy day.

—Helen Boehm

Light tomorrow with today.

—Elizabeth Barrett Browning

Do today's duty, fight today's temptation; do not weaken and distract yourself by looking forward to things you cannot see, and could not understand if you saw them.

—Charles Kingsley

The best preparation for good work
tomorrow is to do good work today.
—Elbert Hubbard

Live for today. Multitudes of people have
failed to live for today.... What they have
had within their grasp today they have
missed entirely, because only the future
has intrigued them.
—William Allen White

Present opportunities are neglected, and
attainable good is slighted, by minds bus-
ied in extensive ranges and intent upon
future advantages.
—Samuel Johnson

A preoccupation with the future not
only prevents us from seeing the present
as it is, but often prompts us to
rearrange the past.
—Eric Hoffer

The man least dependent upon the morrow goes to meet the morrow most cheerfully.

—Epicurus

We steal if we touch tomorrow. It is God's.

—Henry Ward Beecher

Today's egg is better than tomorrow's hen.

—Turkish proverb

T'were too absurd to slight for the hereafter, the day's delight!

—Robert Browning

The best part of our lives we pass in counting on what is to come.

—William Hazlitt

It seems to be the fate of man to seek all his consolations in futurity.

—Samuel Johnson

The prospect of being pleased tomorrow will never console me for the boredom of today.

—Francois de La Rochefoucauld

To live only for some future goal is shallow. It's the sides of the mountain that sustain life, not the top.

—Robert M. Pirsig

The past and present are only our means; the future is always our end. Thus we never really live, but only hope to live.

—Blaise Pascal

PART FOUR

THIS MOMENT

The Preciousness
of Each Moment

Every second is of infinite value.
          —Johann von Goethe

Let me tell thee, time is a very precious
gift of God; so precious that it's only
given to us moment by moment.
          —Amelia Barr

This—this was what made life: a
moment of quiet, the water falling in
the fountain, the girl's voice ... a
moment of captured beauty. He who is
truly wise will never permit such
moments to escape.
          —Louis L'Amour

The span of life is waning fast;
Beware, unthinking youth, beware!
Thy soul's eternity depends
Upon the record moments bear!
          —Eliza Cook

Florence Farr once said to me, "If we could say to ourselves, with sincerity, 'this passing moment is as good as any I shall ever know,' we could die upon the instant and be united with God."

—William Butler Yeats

Sometimes I would almost rather have people take away years of my life than take away a moment.

—Pearl Bailey

We do not remember days, we remember moments.

—Cesare Pavese

Life is a succession of moments. To live each one is to succeed.

—Corita Kent

Life is not lost by dying; life is lost minute by minute, day by day, in all the thousand small, uncaring ways.

—Stephen Saint Vincent Benet

I have the happiness of the passing
moment, and what more can mortal ask?
—George R. Gissing

The sole life which a man can lose is that
which he is living at the moment.
—Marcus Aurelius

I always say to myself, what is the most
important thing we can think about at
this extraordinary moment.
—Francois de La Rochefoucauld

I live now and only now, and I will do
what I want to do this moment and not
what I decided was best for me yesterday.
—Hugh Prather

Fill the unforgiving minute with sixty
seconds worth of distance run.
—Rudyard Kipling

The present moment is creative, creating
with an unheard-of intensity.
—Le Corbusier

But what minutes! Count them by sensation, and not by calendars, and each moment is a day.

—Benjamin Disraeli

The only way to live is to accept each minute as an unrepeatable miracle, which is exactly what it is: a miracle and unrepeatable.

—Storm Jameson

Who makes quick use of the moment is a genius of prudence.

—Johann Kaspar Lavater

Be always resolute with the present hour. Every moment is of infinite value.

—Boethe

To finish the moment, to find the journey's end in every step of the road, to live the greatest number of good hours, is wisdom.

—Ralph Waldo Emerson

God speaks to all individuals through what happens to them moment by moment.

—J.P. DeCaussade

It may be life is only worthwhile at moments. Perhaps that is all we ought to expect.

—Sherwood Anderson

Our latest moment is always our supreme moment. Five minutes delay in dinner now is more important than a great sorrow ten years gone.

—Samuel Butler

A player's effectiveness is directly related to his ability to be right there, doing that thing, in the moment.... He can't be worrying about the past or the future or the crowd or some other extraneous event. He must be able to respond in the here and now.

—John Brodie

OUR MOMENTS PASS TOO QUICKLY

Life is all memory except for the one present moment that goes by so quick you
can hardly catch it going.

—Tennessee Williams

It is privilege of living to be ... acutely,
agonizingly conscious of the moment
that is always present and always passing.

—Marya Mannes

The passing moment is all we can be sure
of; it is only common sense to extract its
utmost value from it.

—W. Somerset Maugham

We have only this moment, sparkling
like a star in our hand ... and melting
like a snowflake. Let us use it before it is
too late.

—Marie Beynon Ray

GENERAL QUOTATIONS ABOUT MOMENTS

We must not wish anything other than what happens from moment to moment, all the while, however, exercising ourselves in goodness.

> —Saint Catherine of Genoa

He is blessed over all mortals who loses no moment of the passing life.

> —Henry David Thoreau

The only courage that matters is the kind that gets you from one moment to the next.

> —Mignon McLaughlin

The moment of change is the only poem.

> —Adrienne Rich

If it weren't for the last minute, nothing would get done.

> —Anon.

Once to every man and nation comes the
    moment to decide....
And the choice goes by forever t'wixt
    that darkness and that light.
                    —James Russell Lowell

Love the moment and the energy of the
moment will spread beyond all bound-
aries.

                    —Corita Kent

PART FIVE

MORNINGS

NO MATTER HOW BAD THINGS LOOK AT NIGHT, THEY USUALLY LOOK BETTER IN THE MORNING

Beware of desp'rate steps; the darkest day
lived till tomorrow will have pass'd away.
—William Cowper

The weariest night, the longest day,
sooner or later must perforce come to an
end.
—Baroness Orczy

Weeping may endure for a night, but joy
cometh in the morning.
—Ps. 30:5

The morning is wiser than the evening.
—Russian proverb

Sadness flies on the wings of the morning, and out of the heart of darkness
comes the light.
—Jean Giraudoux

Out of the scabbard of the night,
By God's hand drawn,
Flashes his shining sword of light,
And lo, the dawn!
                    —Frank Dempster Sherman

Have hope. Though clouds environs
    now,
And gladness hides her face in scorn,
Put thou the shadow from thy brow—
No night but hath its morn.
                    —J.C.F. von Schiller

For the mind disturbed, the still beauty
of dawn is nature's finest balm.
                    —Edwin Way Teale

It is a common experience that a problem difficult at night is resolved in the
morning after the committee of sleep has
worked on it.
                    —John Steinbeck

WE'RE REBORN EACH MORNING

Each day is a new life. Seize it. Live it.
                    —David Guy Powers

Always begin anew with the day, just as
nature does. It is one of the sensible
things that nature does.
                    —George E. Woodberry

With each sunrise, we start anew.
                    —Anon.

We are new every day.
          —Irene Claremont de Castillego

Snow endures but for a season, and joy
comes with the morning.
                    —Marcus Aurelius

Each day the world is born anew for him
who takes it rightly.
                    —James Russell Lowell

146

I have always been delighted at the prospect of a new day, a fresh try, one more start, with perhaps a bit of magic waiting somewhere behind the morning.

—J.B. Priestly

Relying on God has to begin all over again every day as if nothing had yet been done.

—C.S. Lewis

Hold your head high, stick your chest out. You can make it. It gets dark sometimes, but morning comes.... Keep hope alive.

—Jesse Jackson

Have patience with all things, but chiefly have patience with yourself. Do not lose courage in considering your own imperfections, but instantly set about remedying them—every day begin the task anew.

—Saint Francis de Sales

For what human ill does not dawn seem to be an alleviation?
—Thornton Wilder

Each day is a little life; every waking and rising a little birth; every fresh morning a little youth; every going to rest and sleep a little death.
—Arthur Schopenhauer

I love the challenge of starting at zero every day and seeing how much I can accomplish.
—Martha Stewart

Whether one is twenty, forty, or sixty; whether one has succeeded, failed or just muddled along; whether yesterday was full of sun or storm, or one of those dull days with no weather at all, life begins each morning!... Each morning is the open door to a new world—new vistas, new aims, new tryings.
—Leigh Mitchell Hodges

To be seeing the world made new every morning, as if it were the morning of the first day, and then to make the most of it for the individual soul as if each were the last day, is the daily curriculum of the mind's desire.

—John H. Finley

Do not say, "It is morning," and dismiss it with a name of yesterday. See it for the first time as a newborn child that has no name.

—Rabindranath Tagore

God had infinite time to give us.... He cut it up into a near succession of new mornings, and, with each, therefore, a new idea, new inventions, and new applications.

—Ralph Waldo Emerson

GET UP QUICKLY

No matter how big or soft or warm your
bed is, you still have to get out of it.
—Grace Slick

Spill not the morning (the quintessence
of the day!) in recreations, for sleep is a
recreation. Add not, therefore, sauce to
sauce.... Pastime, like wine, is poison in
the morning. It is then good husbandry
to sow the head, which hath lain fallow
all night, with some serious work.
—Thomas Fuller

Do not shorten the morning by getting
up late; look upon it as the quintessence
of life, and to a certain extent sacred.
—Arthur Schopenhauer

Let us then be up and doing, with a
heart for any fate.
—Henry Wadsworth Longfellow

He'd jolt up in bed every morning, sit quietly for a moment, and you could feel those wheels spinning in his mind as he planned his day. Then he'd hit the floor almost on the run.

—Sasha Stallone, describing
Sylvester's early Hollywood days

Get up, stand up; stand up for your rights.

—Bob Marley

Clay lies still, but blood's a rover
Breath's a ware that will not keep.
Up lad: when the journey's over
There'll be time enough to sleep.

—A.E. Housman

Even if a farmer intends to loaf, he gets up in time to get an early start.

—Edgar Watson Howe

GIVE THANKS

I thank You God for this most amazing
day; for the leaping greenly spirits of
trees and a blue true dream of sky; and
for everything which is natural which is
infinite which is yes.

—e.e. cummings

I get up and I bless the light thin clouds
and the first twittering of birds, and the
breathing air and smiling face of the hills.

—Giacomo Leopardi

I'm a most lucky and thankful woman.
Lucky and thankful for each morning I
wake up. For three wonderful daughters
and one son. For an understanding and
very loving husband with whom I've
shared fifty-two blessed years, all in good
health.

—Thelma Elliott

CHOOSING HOW OUR DAY WILL BE

Here we stand between two eternities of
darkness. What are we to do with this
glory while it is still ours?
                              —Gilbert Murray

To get up each morning with the resolve
to be happy ... is to set our own condi-
tions to the events of each day. To do this
is to condition circumstances instead of
being conditioned by them.
                              —Ralph Waldo Trine

The first thing each morning, and the
last thing each night, suggest to yourself
specific ideas that you wish to embody in
your character and personality. Address
such suggestions to yourself, silently or
aloud, until they are deeply impressed
upon your mind.
                              —Grenville Kleiser

Be pleasant until ten o'clock in the morning and the rest of the day will take care of itself.

—Elbert Hubbard

Your morning thoughts may determine your conduct for the day. Optimistic thoughts will make your day bright and productive, while pessimistic thinking will make it dull and wasteful. Face each day cheerfully, smilingly and courageously, and it will naturally follow that your work will be a real pleasure and progress will be a delightful accomplishment.

—William M. Peck

Everyday ask yourself the question, "Do I want to experience Peace of Mind or do I want to experience Conflict?"

—Gerald Jampolsky

When you rise in the morning, form a resolution to make the day a happy one for a fellow creature.

—Sydney Smith

It was only a sunny smile,
And little it cost in the giving.
But like morning light, it scattered the
    night,
And made the day worth living.

—Anon.

Today a thousand doors of enterprise are
open to you, inviting you to useful
work. To live at this time is an ines-
timable privilege, and a sacred obligation
devolves upon you to make right use of
your opportunities. Today is the day in
which to attempt and achieve something
worthwhile.

—Grenville Kleiser

My credo is etched on my mirror in my
bathroom and I see it when I brush my
teeth in the morning. It says, "Don't
worry, Be Happy, Feel Good." When
you see that first thing, and you reflect
on it, the rest of the day seems to glide
by pretty well.

—Larry Hagman

155

Every new day begins with possibilities.
It's up to us to fill it with the things that
move us toward progress and peace.

—Ronald Reagan

Here hath been dawning another blue
day: think, wilt thou let it slip useless
away?

—Thomas Carlyle

Today is a new day. You will get out of it
just what you put into it.... If you have
made mistakes, even serious mistakes,
there is always another chance for you.
And supposing you have tried and failed
again and again, you may have a fresh
start any moment you choose, for this
thing that we call "failure" is not the
falling down, but the staying down.

—Mary Pickford

I think in terms of the day's resolutions,
not the year's.

—Henry Moore

The day returns and brings us the petty
round of irritating concerns and duties.
Help us to play the man, help us to perform them with laughter and kind faces;
let cheerfulness abound with industry.
Give us to go blithely on our business all
this day, bring us to our resting beds
weary and content and undishonored,
and grant us in the end the gift of sleep.
—Robert Louis Stevenson

This is the beginning of a new day. God
has given me this day to use as I will. I
can waste it or use it for good, but what I
do today is important, because I am
exchanging a day of my life for it! When
tomorrow comes, this day will be gone
forever, leaving in its place something that
I have traded for it. I want it to be gain,
and not loss; good, and not evil; success,
and not failure; in order that I shall not
regret the price I have paid for it.
—Anon.

Get out of bed forcing a smile. You may not smile because you are cheerful; but if you will force yourself to smile you'll ... be cheerful because you smile. Repeated experiments prove that when man assumes the facial expression of a given mental mood, any given mood, then that mental mood itself will follow.

—Kenneth Goode

As soon as you open your eyes in the morning, you can square away for a happy and successful day. It's the mood and the purpose at the inception of each day that are the important facts in charting your course for the day. We can always square away for a fresh start, no matter what the past has been.

—George Matthew Adams

One never knows what each day is going to bring. The important thing is to be open and ready for it.

—Henry Moore

He who every morning plans the transactions of the day and follows that plan carries thread that will guide him through the labyrinth of the most busy life.

—Victor Hugo

A man without a plan for the day is lost before he starts.

—Lewis K. Bendele

Only that day dawns to which we are awake.

—Henry David Thoreau

Sometimes I have believed as many as six impossible things before breakfast.

—Lewis Carroll

The mind is found most acute and most uneasy in the morning. Uneasiness is, indeed, a species of sagacity—a passive sagacity. Fools are never uneasy.

—Johann von Goethe

REMAINING OPEN TO UNFORESEEN OPPORTUNITIES AND GIFTS

A day dawns, quite like other days; in it,
a single hour comes, quite like other
hours; but in that day and in that hour
the chance of a lifetime faces us.

—Maltbie Babcock

Great opportunities come to all, but
many do not know they have met them.
The only preparation to take advantage
of them is ... to watch what each day
brings.

—Albert E. Dunning

There will be something, anguish or ela-
tion, that is peculiar to this day alone. I
rise from sleep and say: Hail to the
morning! Come down to me, my beautiful unknown.

—Jessica Powers

THE MORNING SUN

The sun is new each day.

—Heraclitus

With every rising of the sun, think of
your life as just begun.

—Anon.

I feel very happy to see the sun come up
every day. I feel happy to be around.... I
like to take this day—any day—and go
to town with it.

—James Dickey

Each golden sunrise ushers in new
opportunities for those who retain faith
in themselves, and keep their chins up....
Meet the sunrise with confidence. Fill
every golden minute with right thinking
and worthwhile endeavor. Do this and
there will be joy for you in each golden
sunset.

—Alonzo Newton Benn

Today a new sun rises for me; everything lives, everything is animated, everything seems to speak to me of my passion, everything invites me to cherish it.
—Anne De Lenclos

The morning has gold in its mouth.
—German proverb

What humbugs we are, who pretend to live for Beauty, and never see the Dawn!
—Logan Pearsall Smith

Sunrise: day's great progenitor.
—Emily Dickinson

Oft when the white, still dawn lifted the skies and pushed the hills apart, I have felt it like a glory in my heart.
—Edwin Markham

GENERAL QUOTATIONS ABOUT MORNINGS

Put yourself in competition with yourself each day. Each morning look back upon your work of yesterday and then try to beat it.

—Charles M. Sheldon

Do you know what the greatest test is? Do you still get excited about what you do when you get up in the morning?

—David Halberstam

Day's sweetest moments are at dawn.

—Ella Wheeler Wilcox

If God adds another day to our life, let us receive it gladly.

—Marcus Annaeus Seneca

Wake at dawn with a winged heart and give thanks for another day of loving.

—Kahlil Gibran

PART SIX

EVENINGS

NIGHTLY ASSESSMENTS

We should every night call ourselves to
an account: What infirmity have I mas-
tered today? What passions opposed!
What temptation resisted? What virtue
acquired?

—Marcus Annaeus Seneca

Fools look to tomorrow; wise men use
tonight.

—Scottish proverb

Judge each day not by it's harvest, but by
the seeds you plant.

—Anon.

Each morning puts man on trial and
each evening passes judgement.

—Roy L. Smith

I think, what has this day brought me,
and what have I given it?

—Henry Moore

Every night before I turn out the lights
to sleep, I ask myself this question: Have
I done everything that I can.... Have I
done enough?
                    —Lyndon B. Johnson

Each morning sees some task begin, each
    evening sees it close;
Something attempted, something done,
    has earned a night's repose.
                    —Henry Wadsworth Longfellow

Sum up at night what thou has done by
day.
                    —Lord Herbert

One of the secrets of a long and fruitful
life is to forgive everybody everything
every night before you go to bed.
                    —Anon.

Let not the sun go down upon your
wrath.
                    —Eph. 14:26

Taking Off Our Cares
and Negative Emotions
with Our Clothing

Shed, as you do your garments, your
daily sins, whether of omission or com-
mission, and you will wake a free man,
with a new life.

—Sir William Osler

Put off thy cares with thy clothes; so shall
thy rest strengthen thy labor, and so thy
labor sweeten thy rest.

—Francis Quarles

The camel, at the close of day,
Kneels down upon the sandy plain
To have his burden lifted off
And rest again.
My soul, thou too should to thy knees
When daylight draweth to a close,
And let thy Master lift the load
And grant repose.

—Anon.

SLEEP

Thou driftest gently down the tides of
sleep.

> —Henry Wadsworth Longfellow

Go to bed early, get up early—this is
wise.

> —Mark Twain

Come Sleep! Oh Sleep, the certain knot
   of peace,
The baiting-place of wit, the balm of
   woe,
The poor man's wealth, the prisoner's
   release,
The indifferent judge between the high
   and low.

> —Sir Philip Sidney

Health is the first muse, and sleep is the
condition to produce it.

> —Ralph Waldo Emerson

Blessings on him that invented sleep! It covers a man, thoughts and all, like a cloak; it is meat for the hungry, drink for the thirsty, heat for the cold, and cold for the hot. It is the currency with which everything may be purchased, and the balance that sets even king and shepherd, simpleton and sage.

—Miguel de Cervantes

Sleep, that knits up the ravell'd slave of
  care,
The death of each day's life, sore labour's
  bath,
Balm of hurt minds, great nature's second course,
Chief nourisher in life's feast.

—William Shakespeare

O bed! O bed! Delicious bed! That heav-
en on earth to the weary head!

—Thomas Hood

Fatigue is the best pillow.

—Benjamin Franklin

A well-spent day brings happy sleep.
—Leonardo da Vinci

It is a delicious moment, certainly, that of being well-nestled in bed and feeling that you shall drop gently to sleep. The good is to come, not past; the limbs are tired enough to render the remaining in one posture delightful; the labor of the day is gone.
—Leigh Hunt

Sleep, Silence's child, sweet father of soft
    rest,
Prince whose approach peace to all mor-
    tals brings,
Indifferent host to shepherds and kings,
Sole comforter to minds with grief
    oppressed.
—William Drummond

There is only one thing people like that is good for them; a good night's sleep.
—Edgar Watson Howe

Sleep is the most blessed and blessing of all natural graces.

—Aldous Huxley

It is a common experience that a problem difficult at night is resolved in the morning after the committee of sleep has worked on it.

—John Steinbeck

Don't fight with the pillow, but lay down your head
And kick every worriment out of the bed.

—Edmund Vance Cooke

Thank God for sleep! And when you cannot sleep, still thank Him that you live to lie awake.

—John Oxenham

Sleep ... peace of the soul, who puttest care to flight.

—Ovid

Now I lay me down to sleep, I pray the Lord my soul to keep.

—Anon.

There may be those on earth who dress better or eat better, but those who enjoy the peace of God sleep better.

—L. Thomas Holdcroft

Let us add this one more night to our lives.

—Suetonius

To carry care to bed is to sleep with a pack on your back.

—Thomas C. Haliburton

Sleep: The golden chain that ties health and our bodies together.

—Thomas Dekker

PART SEVEN

TOMORROW: THE FUTURE

WE'RE NOT SUPPOSED TO SEE TOO FAR AHEAD

It is a mistake to look too far ahead.
Only one link in the chain of destiny can
be handled at a time.
— Sir Winston Churchill

Neither in the life of the individual nor
in that of mankind is it desirable to
know the future.
— Jakob Burckhardt

God made the world round so we would
never be able to see too far down the
road.
— Isak Dinesen

The future comes one day at a time.
— Dean Acheson

The best thing about the future is that it
comes only one day at a time.
— Abraham Lincoln

There is a case, and a strong case, for that particular form of indolence that allows us to move through life knowing only what immediately concerns us.

—Alec Waugh

Cease to inquire what the future has in store, and take as a gift whatever the day brings forth.

—Horace

There is no data on the future.

—Laurel Cutler

Hardly anyone knows how much is gained by ignoring the future.

—Bernard de Fontenelle

The future is hidden even from those who make it.

—Anatole France

Tomorrow's Always Another Day

Be of good cheer. Do not think of today's failures, but of the success that may come tomorrow. You have set yourselves a difficult task, but you will succeed if you persevere; and you will find a joy in overcoming obstacles. Remember, no effort that we make to attain something beautiful is ever lost.

—Helen Keller

Everyone has it within his power to say, this I am today, that I shall be tomorrow.

—Louis L'Amour

When all else is lost, the future still remains.

—Christian Bovee

I have been nothing ... but there is tomorrow.

—Louis L'Amour

After all, tomorrow is another day.
—Scarlett O'Hara,
Gone With The Wind

They who lose today may win tomorrow.
—Miguel de Cervantes

I am not afraid of tomorrow, for I have
seen yesterday and I love today.
—William Allen White

Yesterday is not ours to recover, but
tomorrow is ours to win or lose.
—Lyndon B. Johnson

The possibilities for tomorrow are usually
beyond our expectations.
—Anon.

Take therefore no thought of the morrow; for the morrow shall take thought
for the things of itself.
—Mt. 6:34

We Can't Be Afraid
of the Future

He who foresees calamities suffers them
twice over.

> —Beilby Porteous

Only man clogs his happiness with care,
destroying what is with thoughts of what
may be.

> —John Dryden

If you are afraid for your future, you
don't have a present.

> —James Petersen

He that fears not the future may enjoy
the present.

> —Thomas Fuller

Cowards die many times before their
deaths; the valiant never taste of death
but once.

> —William Shakespeare

We need not be afraid of the future, for the future will be in our own hands.
—Thomas E. Dewey

The future is called "perhaps," which is the only possible thing to call the future. And the important thing is not to allow that to scare you.
—Tennessee Williams

The mere apprehension of a coming evil has put many into a situation of the utmost danger.
—Lucan

It is never safe to look into the future with eyes of fear.
—E.H. Harriman

Nothing in life is more remarkable than the unnecessary anxiety which we endure, and generally create ourselves.
—Benjamin Disraeli

To relinquish a present good through apprehension of a future evil is in most instances unwise ... from a fear which may afterwards turn out groundless, you lost the good that lay within your grasp.
—Francesco Guicciardini

Every man, through fear, mugs his aspirations a dozen times a day.
—Brendan Francis

Go forth to meet the shadowy Future without fear and with a manly heart.
—Henry Wadsworth Longfellow

We grow in time to trust the future for our answers.
—Ruth Benedict

Every tomorrow has two handles. We can take hold of it with the handle of anxiety or the handle of faith.
—Henry Ward Beecher

Put aside the need to know some future design and simply leave your life open to what is needed of it by the Divine forces.

—Emmanuel

The only limit to our realization of tomorrow will be our doubts of today. Let us move forward with strong and active faith.

—Franklin Delano Roosevelt

It is not the cares of today, but the cares of tomorrow, that weigh a man down. For the needs of today we have corresponding strength given. For the morrow we are told to trust. It is not ours yet.

—George MacDonald

To the being of fully alive, the future is not ominous but a promise; it surrounds the present like a halo.

—John Dewey

OTHER DEFINITIONS OF TOMORROW AND THE FUTURE

Tomorrow is the day when idlers work, and fools reform, and mortal men lay hold on heaven.

—Edward Young

Tomorrow is the mysterious, unknown guest.

—Henry Wadsworth Longfellow

Tomorrow is the only day in the year that appeals to a lazy man.

—Jimmy Lyons

The future is something which everyone reaches at the rate of sixty minutes an hour, whatever he does, whoever he is.

—C.S. Lewis

The future is the most expensive luxury in the world.

—Thornton Wilder

The future is a world limited by ourselves—in it we discover only what concerns us.

—Maurice Maeterlinck

The future is only the past again, entered
through another gate.

—Arthur Wing Pinero

The future is the shape of things to
come.

—H. G. Wells

The future is the past in preparation.

—Pierre Dac

The future is hope!

—John Fiske

The future is a great land.

—Anon.

The future is wider than vision, and has
no end.

—Donald G. Mitchell

General Quotations about Tomorrow and the Future

Grow old along with me! The best is yet to be.

—Robert Browning

He who lives in the future lives in a featureless blank; he lives in impersonality; he lives in Nirvana. The past is democratic, because it is a people. The future is despotic, because it is a caprice. Every man is alone in his prediction, just as each man is alone in a dream.

—G.K. Chesterton

The future belongs to those who believe in the beauty of their dreams.

—Eleanor Roosevelt

I like the dreams of the future better than the history of the past.

—Thomas Jefferson

You cannot plan the future by the past.
—Edmund Burke

It is when tomorrow's burden is added to the burden of today that the weight is more than a man can bear.
—George MacDonald

My interest is in the future because I am going to spend the rest of my life there.
—Charles F. Kettering

I never think of the future. It comes soon enough.
—Albert Einstein

Where will I be five years from now? I delight in not knowing. That's one of the greatest things about life—its wonderful surprises.
—Marlo Thomas

When I look at the future, it's so bright, it burns my eyes.
—Oprah Winfrey

Everyone's future is, in reality, uncertain
and full of unknown treasures from
which all may draw unguessed prizes.
                    —Lord Dunsany

The future is made of the same stuff as
the present.
                    —Simone Weil

By-and-by never comes.
                    —Saint Augustine

For you and me, today is all we have;
tomorrow is a mirage that may never
become reality.
                    —Louis L'Amour

The bridges you cross before you come
to them are over rivers that aren't there.
                    —Gene Brown

Strike when thou wilt, the hour of rest,
but let my last days be my best.
                    —Robert Browning

If a man carefully examines his thoughts he will be surprised to find how much he lives in the future. His well-being is always ahead.

—Ralph Waldo Emerson

I got the blues thinking of the future, so I left off and made some marmalade. It's amazing how it cheers one up to shred oranges and scrub the floor.

—D.H. Lawrence

You learn to build your roads on today, because tomorrow's ground is too uncertain for plans, and futures have a way of falling down in mid-flight.

—Veronica Shoffstal

Fortunately for children, the uncertainties of the present always give way to the enchanted possibilities of the future.

—Gelsey Kirkland

PART EIGHT

AVERAGE DAYS

AVERAGE DAYS

Normal day, let me be aware of the treasure you are. Let me learn from you, love you, bless you before you depart. Let me not pass you by in quest of some rare and perfect tomorrow. Let me hold you while I may, for it may not always be so. One day I shall dig my nails into the earth, or bury my face in the pillow, or stretch myself taut, or raise my hands to the sky and want, more than all the world, your return.

—Mary Jean Iron

Either you reach a higher point today, or you exercise your strength in order to be able to climb higher tomorrow.

—Friedrich Nietzsche

That man is happiest who lives from day to day and asks no more, garnering the simple goodness of a life.

—Euripides

One appreciates that daily life is really good when one wakes from a horrible dream, or when one takes the first outing after a sickness. Why not realize it now?

     —William Lyon Phelps

Write it on your heart that every day is the best day in the year.

     —Ralph Waldo Emerson

Sunshine is delicious, rain is refreshing, wind braces us, snow is exhilarating; there is no such thing as bad weather, only different kinds of good weather.

     —John Ruskin

This is the day which the Lord hath made; we will rejoice and be glad.

     —Ps. 118:24

We do not live an equal life, but one of contrasts and patchwork; now a little joy, then a sorrow, now a sin, then a generous or brave action.

     —Ralph Waldo Emerson

DAY-TO-DAY LIVING IS HARDER THAN AN EMERGENCY

Peace hath higher tests of manhood
Than battle ever knew.

>   —John Greenleaf Whittier

Poets are like baseball pitchers. Both have
their moments. The intervals are the
tough things.

>   —Robert Frost

Man lives by habits indeed, but what he
lives for is thrill and excitements.... From
time immemorial war has been ... the
supremely thrilling excitement.

>   —William James

We look wishfully to emergencies, to
eventful, revolutionary times ... and
think how easy to have taken our part
when the drum was rolling and the
house was burning over our heads.

>   —Ralph Waldo Emerson

A man can stand almost anything except
a succession of ordinary days.
—Johann von Goethe

Peace is not only better than war, but
infinitely more arduous.
—George Bernard Shaw

Any idiot can face a crisis—it's day to
day living that wears you out.
—Anton Chekhov

They sicken of the calm that know the
storm.
—Ralph Waldo Emerson

It is not merely cruelty that leads men to
love war, it is excitement.
—Henry Ward Beecher

The statistics of suicide show that, for
non-combatants at least, life is more
interesting in war than in peace.
—William Ralph Inge

THE PROBLEMS AND DANGERS
OF BOREDOM

Boredom is rage spread thin.
                                —Paul Tillich

One of the worst forms of mental suffering is boredom, not knowing what to do
with oneself and one's life. Even if man
had no monetary, or any other reward,
he would be eager to spend his energy in
some meaningful way because he could
not stand the boredom which inactivity
produces.
                                —Erich Fromm

Boredom is the most horrible of wolves.
                                —Jean Giono

Ennui has made more gamblers than
avarice, more drunkards than thirst, and
perhaps as many suicides as despair.
                          —Charles Caleb Colton

Boredom ... causes us to neglect more duties than does interest.
>—Francois de La Rochefoucauld

Boredom is a vital problem for the moralist, since at least half of the sins of mankind are caused by the fear of it.
>—Bertrand Russell

Boredom slays more of existence than war.
>—Norman Mailer

Monotony is the awful reward of the careful.
>—A.G. Buckham

One must choose in life between boredom and suffering.
>—Madame de Stael

The only menace is inertia.
>—Saint John Perse

WE BORE OURSELVES, AND IT'S UP TO US TO OVERCOME BOREDOM

If your daily life seems poor, do not blame it; blame yourself, tell yourself that you are not poet enough to call forth its riches.

—Rainer Maria Rilke

When people are bored, it is primarily with their own selves that they are bored.

—Eric Hoffer

Nothing is interesting if you're not interested.

—Helen MacInness

Is not life a hundred times too short for us to bore ourselves?

—Friedrich Nietzsche

Somebody's boring me; I think it's me.

—Dylan Thomas

Being bored is an insult to oneself.

—Jules Renard

The amount of satisfaction you get from life depends largely on your own ingenuity, self-sufficiency, and resourcefulness. People who wait around for life to supply their satisfaction usually find boredom instead.

—Dr. William Menninger

Boredom is a sickness of the soul.

—Anon.

Boredom is simply the lack of imagination.

—Julie O. Smith

Perhaps the world's second worst crime is boredom. The first is being a bore.

—Cecil Beaton

SOME REMEDIES FOR BOREDOM

In the ancient recipe, the three antidotes for dullness or boredom are sleep, drink, and travel. It is rather feeble. From sleep you wake up, from drink you become sober, and from travel you come home again. And then where are you? No, the two sovereign remedies for dullness are love or a crusade.

—D.H. Lawrence

If something is boring after two minutes, try it for four. If still boring, try it for eight, sixteen, thirty-two, and so on. Eventually, one discovers that it is not boring, but very interesting.

—Zen saying

Nobody is bored when he is trying to make something that is beautiful, or to discover something that is true.

—William Ralph Inge

As for boredom ... I notice that it leaves me as soon as I am doing something that has got to be done.

—John Jay Chapman

The one sure means of dealing with boredom is to care for someone else, to do something kind and good.

—Theodore Haecker

Everything considered, work is less boring than amusing oneself.

—Charles Baudelaire

Boredom, like necessity, is very often the mother of invention.

—Anon.

Uncertainty and mystery are energies of life. Don't let them scare you unduly, for they keep boredom at bay and spark creativity.

—R.I. Fitzbenry

GENERAL QUOTATIONS
ABOUT BOREDOM

Man is the only animal that can be bored.

—Erich Fromm

The only unhappiness is a life of boredom.

—Stendhal

It is better to be happy for the moment and be burned up with beauty than to live a long time and be bored all the while.

—Don Marquis

One can be bored until boredom becomes a mystical experience.

—Logan Pearsall Smith

We often forgive those who bore us, but can't forgive those whom we bore.

—Francois de La Rochefoucauld

Dullness is a misdemeanor.

—Ethel Wilson

Boredom is useful to me when I notice it and think: Oh I'm bored; there must be something else I want to be doing ... boredom acts as an initiator of originality by pushing me into new activities or new thoughts.

—Hugh Prather

Life is as tedious as a twice-told tale, vexing the dull ear of a drowsy man.

—William Shakespeare

One of man's finest qualities is described by the simple word "guts"—the ability to take it. If you have the discipline to stand fast when your body wants to run, if you can control your temper and remain cheerful in the face of monotony or disappointments, you have "guts" in the soldiering sense.

—Colonel John S. Roosman

Three-quarters of a soldier's life is spent
in aimlessly waiting about.
—Eugene Rosenstock-Huessy

Boredom: the desire for desires.
—Leo Tolstoy

Overexcitement and boredom are states
of mind which I equally shun.
—E.V. Knox

An enthusiast may bore others, but he
has never a dull moment himself.
—John Kieran

Passions are less mischievous than boredom, for passions tend to diminish and
boredom increase.
—Barbey d'Aurevilly

PART NINE

DIFFICULT DAYS

DIFFICULT DAYS

Everyone gets their rough day. No one gets a free ride. Today so far, I had a good day. I got a dial tone.

—Rodney Dangerfield

Thy fate is the common fate of all,
Into each life some rain must fall,
Some days must be dark and dreary.

—Henry Wadsworth Longfellow

Some days you tame the tiger. And some days the tiger has you for lunch.

—Tug McGraw

Some days the dragon wins.

—Anon.

He that can't endure the bad will not live to see the good.

—Yiddish proverb

EVERYTHING CHANGES

If matters go badly now, they will not always be so.

—Horace

I don't think that ... one gets a flash of happiness once, and never again; it is there within you, and it will come as certainly as death....

—Isak Dinesen

I feel successful when the writing goes well. This lasts five minutes. Once, when I was number one on the best-seller list, I also felt successful. That lasted three minutes.

—Jacqueline Briskin

Experience cold or heat, pleasure or pain. These experiences are fleeting; they come and go. Bear them patiently.

—Sri Krishna (Bhagavad Gita)

To those who shall sit here rejoicing, and
to those who shall sit here lamenting,
greetings and sympathy. So have we done
in our time.
>   —Bench inscription,
>   Cornell University

Let nothing disturb thee,
Let nothing affright thee,
All things are passing,
God changeth never.
>   —Henry Wadsworth Longfellow

Sadness and gladness succeed each other.
>   —Anon.

Sadness flies away on the wings of time.
>   —Jean de La Fontaine

This, too, shall pass.
>   —William Shakespeare

The present will not long endure.
>   —Pindar

The one law that does not change is that everything changes, and the hardship I was bearing today was only a breath away from the pleasures I would have tomorrow, and those pleasures would be all the richer because of the memories of this I was enduring.

—Louis L'Amour

Life comes in clusters, clusters of solitude, then clusters when there is hardly time to breathe.

—May Sarton

I've never been poor, only broke. Being poor is a frame of mind. Being broke is a temporary situation.

—Mike Todd

Time cools, time clarifies; no mood can be maintained quite unaltered through the course of hours.

—Thomas Mann

209

THE CONDITIONS OF OUR LIVES
CHANGE LIKE NATURE'S SEASONS

If winter comes, can spring be far
behind?

>—Percy Bysshe Shelley

Human misery must somewhere have a
stop; there is no wind that always blows a
storm.

>—Euripides

No winter lasts forever; no spring skips
its turn.

>—Hal Borland

There are trees that seem to die at the
end of autumn. There are also the ever-
greens.

>—Gilbert Maxwell

Sitting quietly, doing nothing, Spring
comes, and the grass grows by itself.

>—*The Gospel According to Zen*

Our Lord has written the promise of resurrection, not in books alone, but in every leaf in springtime.

—Martin Luther

For, lo, the winter is past, the rain is over and gone; the flowers appear on the earth.

—Song 2:11–12

There ain't no cloud so thick that the sun ain't shinin' on t'other side.

—Rattlesnake,
an 1870s mountain man

Time is like a river of fleeting events, and its current is strong; as soon as something comes into sight, it is swept past us, and something else takes its place, and that too will be swept away.

—Marcus Aurelius

PAIN AND SUFFERING

Pain is never permanent.
> —Saint Teresa of Avila

You will suffer and you will hurt. You
will have joy and you will have peace.
> —Alison Cheek

Pain is part of being alive, and we need
to learn that. Pain does not last forever,
nor is it necessarily unbearable, and we
need to be taught that.
> —Rabbi Harold Kushner

Pain is hard to bear....
But with patience, day by day,
Even this shall pass away.
> —Theodore Tilton

Everything in life that we really accept
undergoes a change. So suffering must
become love. That is the mystery.
> —Katherine Mansfield

GOOD THINGS OFTEN RESULT FROM DIFFICULT THINGS

In the darkest hour the soul is replenished and given strength to continue and endure.

> —Heart Warrior Chosa

Our toil is sweet with thankfulness,
Our burden is our boon;
The curse of earth's gray morning is
The blessing of its noon.

> —John Greenleaf Whittier

Were it possible for us to see further than our knowledge reaches, perhaps we would endure our sadnesses with greater confidence than our joys. For they are moments when something new has entered into us, something unknown.

> —Rainer Maria Rilke

Endings Are Also Beginnings

What we call the beginning is often an end. And to make an end is to make a beginning. The end is where we start from.

—T.S. Eliot

When one door of happiness closes, another opens; but often we look so long at the closed door that we do not see the one which has been opened for us.

—Helen Keller

The world is round, and the place which may seem like the end may also be only the beginning.

—Ivy Baker Priest

The crisis of today is the joke of tomorrow.

—H.G. Wells

SOMEDAY, WE'LL LOOK BACK AND THINGS WON'T SEEM AS DIFFICULT AS THEY DO NOW

Perhaps someday it will be pleasant to remember even this.

—Virgil

One day in retrospect the years of struggle will strike you as the most beautiful.

—Sigmund Freud

I've been failing for, like, ten or eleven years. When it turns, it'll turn. Right now I'm just tryin' to squeeze through a very tight financial period, get the movie out, and put my things in order.

—Francis Ford Coppola

Sometimes I found that in my happy moments I could not believe that I had ever been miserable.

—Joanna Field

IT JUST TAKES TIME

Time, in the turning-over of days, works
change, for better or worse.

—Pindar

Time brings all things to pass.

—Aeschylus

Time bears away all things.

—Virgil

Come what come may, time and the
hour runs through the roughest day.

—William Shakespeare

Sadness flies away on the wings of time.

—Jean de La Fontaine

We undo ourselves by impatience.
Misfortunes have their life and their limits, their sickness and their health.

—Michel de Montaigne

The future is something which everyone
reaches at the rate of sixty minutes an
hour, whatever he does, whoever he is.
—C.S. Lewis

That's the advantage of having lived
sixty-five years. You don't feel the need to
be impatient any longer.
—Thornton Wilder

Your three best doctors are faith, time,
and patience.
—From a fortune cookie

Wisely and slow. They stumble that run
fast.
—William Shakespeare

Genius is eternal patience.
—Michelangelo

Genius is nothing but a greater aptitude
for patience.
—Benjamin Franklin

PATIENCE IS A KEY TO SUCCESS, TO VICTORY

Who longest waits most surely wins.
> —Helen Hunt Jackson

Patience is a bitter plant, but it has sweet fruit.
> —German proverb

And he shall reign a goodly king
And sway his hand o'er every clime
With peace writ on his signet ring,
Who bides his time.
> —James Whitcomb Riley

He that can have patience can have what he will.
> —Benjamin Franklin

Adopt the pace of nature, her secret is patience.
> —Ralph Waldo Emerson

Everything comes if a man will only wait.
—Benjamin Disraeli

How poor are they that have not patience? What wound did ever heal but by degrees?
—William Shakespeare

All things come round to him who will but wait.
—Henry Wadsworth Longfellow

It takes time to succeed because success is merely the natural reward of taking time to do anything well.
—Joseph Ross

Patience and fortitude conquer all things.
—Ralph Waldo Emerson

Be not afraid of growing slowly, be afraid only of standing still.
—Chinese proverb

No great thing is created suddenly, any more than a bunch of grapes or a fig. If you tell me that you desire a fig, I answer you that there must be time. Let it first blossom, then bear fruit, then ripen.

—Epictetus

Time deals gently only with those who take it gently.

—Anatole France

Hold on; hold fast; hold out. Patience is genius.

—Georges de Buffon

All human wisdom is summed up in two words: wait and hope.

—Alexandre Dumas

Serene I fold my hands and wait.

—John Burroughs

The race is not to the swift, nor the battle to the strong.

—Eccl. 9:11

Being Productive While
We're Being Patient

Everything comes to him who hustles
while he waits.

> —Thomas A. Edison

The secret of patience ... to do something else in the meantime.

> —Anon.

Have patience with all things, but chiefly
have patience with yourself. Do not lose
courage in considering your own imperfections, but instantly set about remedying them—every day begin the task
anew.

> —Saint Francis de Sales

Let us then be up and doing,
With a heart for any fate,
Still achieving, still pursuing,
Learn to labor and to wait.

> —Henry Wadsworth Longfellow

GENERAL QUOTATIONS ABOUT
DIFFICULT DAYS

God will wait as long as it takes for us.
—Reverend R. Walters

Who bides his time tastes the sweet
Of honey in the saltiest tear;
And though he fares with slowest feet
Joy runs to meet him drawing near.
—James Whitcomb Riley

Waiting is not mere empty hoping. It has
the inner certainty of reaching the goal.
—I Ching

There is nothing so bitter that a patient
mind cannot find some solace for it.
—Marcus Annaeus Seneca

All things come to him who waits—pro-
vided he knows what he is waiting for.
—Woodrow Wilson

Hope and patience are two sovereign remedies for all, the surest reposals, the softest cushions to lean on in adversity.
— Robert Burton

The strongest of all warriors are these two—Time and Patience.
— Leo Tolstoy

Better is the end of a thing than the beginning thereof: and the patient in spirit is better than the proud in spirit.
— Eccl. 7:8

For ye have need of patience....
— Heb. 10:36

God grant us patience!
— William Shakespeare

They are ill discoverers that think there is no land, when they see nothing but sea.
— Francis Bacon

PART TEN

ONE STEP AT A TIME

Big Things Are Accomplished One Step at a Time

When you have a great and difficult task, something perhaps almost impossible, if you only work a little at a time, every day a little, suddenly the work will finish itself.

—Isak Dinesen

Nothing is particularly hard if you divide it into small jobs.

—Henry Ford

Look at a stone cutter hammering away at his rock, perhaps a hundred times without as much as a crack showing in it. Yet at the hundred-and-first blow it will split in two, and I know it was not the last blow that did it, but all that had gone before.

—Jacob A. Riis

Not to go back is somewhat to advance. And men must walk, at least, before they dance.

—Alexander Pope

Great things are not done by impulse, but by a series of small things brought together.

—Vincent van Gogh

Well-being is attained little by little, and is no little thing itself.

—Zeno of Citium

Bigness comes from doing many small things well.... Individually, they are not very dramatic transactions. Together, though, they add up.

—Edward S. Finkelstein

If you only keep adding little by little, it will soon become a big heap.

—Hesiod

He who would learn to fly one day
must first learn to stand and walk and
run and climb and dance; one cannot
fly into flying.

—Friedrich Nietzsche

All that I have accomplished ... has been
by that plodding, patient, persevering
process of accretion which builds the ant
heap particle by particle, thought by
thought, fact by fact.

—Elihu Burritt

Many things which cannot be overcome
when they are together, yield themselves
up when taken little by little.

—Plutarch

Much rain wears the marble.

—William Shakespeare

Yesterday I dared to struggle. Today I
dare to win.

—Bernadette Devlin

True worth is doing each day some little good, not dreaming of great things to do by and by.

—Anon.

Little by little does the trick.

—Aesop

It is by attempting to reach the top at a single leap that so much misery is caused in the world.

—William Cobbett

I think and think for months, for years. Ninety-nine times the conclusion is false. The hundredth time I am right.

—Albert Einstein

Many strokes overthrow the tallest oaks.

—John Luly

One thing at a time, all things in succession. That which grows slowly endures.

—J.G. Hubbard

Little drops of water, little grains of sand,
Make the mighty ocean, and the pleasant
    land:
So the little minutes, humble though
    they be,
Make the mighty ages of eternity.
Little deeds of kindness, little words of
    love,
Help to make earth happy, like Heaven
    up above.

—Julia Carney

It is a mistake to look too far ahead.
Only one link in the chain of destiny can
be handled at a time.

—Sir Winston Churchill

A successful individual typically sets his
next goal somewhat, but not too much,
above his last achievement.

—Kurt Lewin

SMALL STEPS ARE BIG DEALS

One sits down first; one thinks afterwards.

—Jean Cocteau

The way a chihuahua goes about eating
a dead elephant is to take a bite and be
very present with that bite. In spiritual
growth, the definitive act is to take one
step and let tomorrow's step take care of
itself!

—William H. Houff

Many strokes, though with a little axe,
hew down and fell the hardest-timber'd
oak.

—William Shakespeare

You don't just luck into things.... You
build step by step, whether it's friend-
ships or opportunities.

—Barbara Bush

Progress is the sum of small victories won by individual human beings.

—Bruce Catton

The waters wear the stones.

—Jb. 14:19

One step and then another, and the
    longest walk is ended.
One stitch and then another, and the
    longest rent is mended.
One brick upon another, and the tallest
    wall is made.
One flake and then another, and the
    deepest snow is laid.

—Anon.

If we take care of the inches, we will not have to worry about the miles.

—Hartley Coleridge

What saves a man is to take a step. Then another step.

—Antoine de Saint-Exupery

Victory is won not in miles, but in inches. Win a little now, hold your ground, and later win a little more.

—Louis L'Amour

Inches make a champion.

—Vince Lombardi

Yard by yard, it's very hard. But inch by inch, it's a cinch.

—Anon.

When Ty Cobb got on first base he had an apparently nervous habit of kicking the bag.... By kicking the bag hard enough Cobb could move it a full two inches closer to second base. He figured that this improved his chances for a steal, or for reaching second base safely on a hit.

—Norman Vincent Peale

LITTLE THINGS ARE BIG THINGS

Most people would succeed in small things if they were not troubled with great ambitions.

—Henry Wadsworth Longfellow

Life is made up of little things. It is very rarely that an occasion is offered for doing a great deal at once. True greatness consists in being great in little things.

—Charles Simmons

Life is a great bundle of little things.

—Oliver Wendell Holmes

Nothing can be done except little by little.

—Charles Baudelaire

Practice yourself in little things, and thence proceed to greater.

—Epictetus

Those people work more wisely who seek to achieve good in their own small corner of the world ... than those who are forever thinking that life is in vain, unless one can ... do big things.

—Herbert Butterfield

I recommend you to take care of the minutes, for the hours will take care of themselves.

—Lord Chesterfield

You've got to think about "big things" while you're doing small things, so that all the small things go in the right direction.

—Alvin Toffler

Trifles make up the happiness or the misery of mortal life.

—Alexander Smith

Little strokes fell great oaks.

—Benjamin Franklin

Take your needle, my child, and work at your pattern; it will come out a rose by and by. Life is like that; one stitch at a time taken patiently, and the pattern will come out all right, like embroidery.
                              —Oliver Wendell Holmes

Most of us miss out on life's big prizes. The Pulitzer. The Nobel. Oscars. Tonys. Emmys. But we're all eligible for life's small pleasures. A pat on the back. A kiss behind the ear. A four-pound bass. A full moon. An empty parking space. A crackling fire. A great meal. A glorious sunset. Hot Soup. Cold beer. Don't fret about copping life's grand awards. Enjoy its tiny delights. There are plenty for all of us.
                              —United Technologies
                              Corporation advertisement

Why not learn to enjoy the little things—there are so many of them.
                              —Anon.

The mere sense of living is joy enough.
—Emily Dickinson

It was only a sunny smile,
But it scattered the night
And little it cost in the giving;
Like morning light,
And made the day worth living.

—Anon.

The big things that come our way are ...
the fruit of seeds planted in the daily
routine of our work.
—William Feather

Human felicity is produced not so much
by great pieces of good fortune that seldom happen as by little advantages that
occur every day.
—Benjamin Franklin

Even a small star shines in the darkness.
—Finnish proverb

How far that little candle throws his beams! So shines a good deed in a naughty world.

—William Shakespeare

It is better to light a candle than to curse the darkness.

—Chinese proverb

If you don't enjoy getting up and working and finishing your work and sitting down to a meal with family or friends, then the chances are you're not going to be happy. If someone bases his happiness or unhappiness on major events like a great new job, huge amounts of money, a flawlessly happy marriage or a trip to Paris, that person isn't going to be happy much of the time. If, on the other hand, happiness depends on a good breakfast, flowers in the yard, a drink or a nap, then we are more likely to live with quite a bit of happiness.

—Andy Rooney

The little things are infinitely the most important.

—Sir Arthur Conan Doyle

Enjoy the little things, for one day you may look back and realize they were the big things.

—Robert Brault

It is in trifles, and when he is off his guard, that a man best shows his character.

—Arthur Schopenhauer

Life is denied by lack of attention, whether it be to cleaning windows or trying to write a masterpiece.

—Nadia Boulanger

Sometimes the littlest things in life are the hardest to take. You can sit on a mountain more comfortably than on a tack.

—Anon.

Put your heart, mind, intellect, and soul even to your smallest acts. This is the secret of success.

—Swami Sivananda

The smallest effort is not lost,
Each wavelet on the ocean tost
Aids in the ebb-tide or the flow;
Each rain-drop makes some floweret
   blow;
Each struggle lessens human woe.

—Charles Mackay

He that is faithful in that which is least is faithful also in much; and he that is unjust in the least is unjust also in much.

—Lk. 16:10

We think in generalities, but we live in detail.

—Alfred North Whitehead

Just Doing Whatever We Can Is Enough

I cannot do everything, but still I can do something; and because I cannot do everything, I will not refuse to do something that I can do.

—Edward Everett Hale

We cannot do everything at once, but we can do something at once.

—Calvin Coolidge

Nobody makes a greater mistake than he who did nothing because he could only do a little.

—Edmund Burke

We must not ... ignore the small daily differences we can make which, over time, add up to big differences that we often cannot foresee.

—Marian Write Edelman